Women's Stage Monologues
of 1999

Other books by Jocelyn A. Beard

100 Men's Stage Monologues from the 1980s
100 Women's Stage Monologues from the 1980s
The Best Men's/Women's Stage Monologues of 1990
The Best Men's/Women's Stage Monologues of 1991
The Best Men's/Women's Stage Monologues of 1992
The Best Men's/Women's Stage Monologues of 1993
The Best Men's/Women's Stage Monologues of 1994
The Best Men's/Women's Stage Monologues of 1995
The Best Men's/Women's Stage Monologues of 1996
The Best Men's/Women's Stage Monologues of 1997
The Best Stage Scenes for Men from the 1980s
The Best Stage Scenes for Women from the 1980s
The Best Stage Scenes of 1992
The Best Stage Scenes of 1993
The Best Stage Scenes of 1994
The Best Stage Scenes of 1995
The Best Stage Scenes of 1996
The Best Stage Scenes of 1997
The Best Stage Scenes of 1998
Monologues from Classic Plays 468 B.C. to 1960 A.D.
Scenes from Classic Plays 468 B.C. to 1970 A.D.
100 Great Monologues from the Renaissance Theatre
100 Great Monologues from the Neo-Classical Theatre
100 Great Monologues from the 19th C. Romantic & Realistic Theatre

Smith and Kraus *Books For Actors*
THE MONOLOGUE SERIES
The Best Men's / Women's Stage Monologues of 1998
The Best Men's / Women's Stage Monologues of 1997
The Best Men's / Women's Stage Monologues of 1996
The Best Men's / Women's Stage Monologues of 1995
The Best Men's / Women's Stage Monologues of 1994
The Best Men's / Women's Stage Monologues of 1993
The Best Men's / Women's Stage Monologues of 1992
The Best Men's / Women's Stage Monologues of 1991
The Best Men's / Women's Stage Monologues of 1990
One Hundred Men's / Women's Stage Monologues from the 1980s
2 Minutes and Under: Character Monologues for Actors
Street Talk: Character Monologues for Actors
Uptown: Character Monologues for Actors
Ice Babies in Oz: Character Monologues for Actors
Monologues from Contemporary Literature: Volume I
Monologues from Classic Plays
100 Great Monologues from the Renaissance Theatre
100 Great Monologues from the Neo-Classical Theatre
100 Great Monologues from the 19th C. Romantic and Realistic Theatres
A Brave and Violent Theatre: 20th C. Irish Monologues, Scenes & Hist. Context
Kiss and Tell: Restoration Monologues, Scenes and Historical Context
The Great Monologues from the Humana Festival
The Great Monologues from the EST Marathon
The Great Monologues from the Women's Project
The Great Monologues from the Mark Taper Forum
YOUNG ACTOR SERIES
Great Scenes and Monologues for Children
Great Monologues for Young Actors
Multicultural Monologues for Young Actors
SCENE STUDY SERIES
Scenes From Classic Plays 468 B.C. to 1960 A.D.
The Best Stage Scenes of 1998
The Best Stage Scenes of 1997
The Best Stage Scenes of 1996
The Best Stage Scenes of 1995
The Best Stage Scenes of 1994
The Best Stage Scenes of 1993
The Best Stage Scenes of 1992
The Best Stage Scenes for Men / Women from the 1980s

If you require prepublication information about upcoming Smith and Kraus
books, you may receive our semiannual catalogue, free of charge, by sending
your name and address to *Smith and Kraus Catalogue, 4 Lower Mill Road, North
Stratford, NH 03590. Or call us at (800) 895-4331, fax (603) 643-1831.*

The Best
Women's Stage Monologues
of 1999

edited by Jocelyn A. Beard

The Monologue Audition Series

SK
A Smith and Kraus Book

Published by Smith and Kraus, Inc.
177 Lyme Road, Hanover, NH 03755

First Edition: February 2001
10 9 8 7 6 5 4 3 2 1

The Monologue Audition Series ISSN 1067-134X

NOTE: These monologues are intended to be used for audition and class study; permission is not required to use the material for those purposes. However, if there is a paid performance of any of the monologues included in this book, please refer to the permissions acknowledgment pages to locate the source who can grant permission for public performance.

Contents

Preface, Jocelyn A. Beard vii

A.B.C. or The Man in the Red Flannel Suit, Leslie Bramm (2). . 1
The Adulterer, Jussi Wahlgren 5
Alchemy, Linda Wilkinson 7
Are You All Right in There?, David-Matthew Barnes. 12
Bad Buddhists, Robert Vivian 15
The Belles of the Mill, Rachel Rubin Ladutke. 16
Bitch, Elizabeth Ruiz (2) 18
Blood Sky, Yasmine Rana. 22
The Blueberry Café, Women at Play, Ann Roth (2) 24
Blue Skies Forever, Claire Braz-Valentine (2) 29
The "B" Word, Dolores Whiskeyman 34
The Connie Saxon Show, Ethan Kanfer 39
Darla, Christopher Woods 42
Eat the Breast, Lindsay Price (2) 44
Echoes from the Street, Corey Tyler (2). 49
Eulogy: What I Would Have Said, Given the Gift of Articulation,
     Daphne R. Hull (2). 53
Eve of Crimes: Memory Motel, Bob Jude Ferrante. 58
Eye of the Beholder, Heidi Decker 62
The Imp of the Perverse, Tami Canaday 64
Jane: Abortion and the Underground, Paula Kamen (2) 66
Killers, Werner Trieschmann. 72
Listening to Insomnia, Amy Beth Arkawy 73
Mercy Falls, Jeni Mahoney 75
Moonshades, Wayne Paul Mattingly 77
The Most Fabulous Story Ever Told, Paul Rudnick 79
My Vicious Angel, Christine Evans 81
Never the Same Rhyme Twice, Rooster Mitchell 83

Officer Justice, Janet Pound 85
Party Store Prisoner, Janet Pound 87
The Power of Love, Sebastian Michael (3) 89
The Quarterly, Valerie von Rosenvinge 97
Rage Amongst Yourselves, Amy Beth Arkawy 99
The Rim of the Wheel, Daphne R. Hull (2) 101
The Serpent's Kiss, Jocelyn Beard (2) 105
Shoes, Sky Vogel 110
Small Mercies, Heidi Decker 112
Sweet Butterfly on an Alligator's Lip, Richard Lay 113
A Third of Your Life, Justin Warner 114
Threnody, David-Matthew Barnes 116
Vernon Early, Horton Foote (2) 118
Wash Out, S. Heide Arbitter 122
What Corbin Knew, Jeffrey Hatcher (2) 124
When Will I Dance, Claire Braz-Valentine 128
Women Behind the Walls, Claire Braz-Valentine (3) 130
Zoë's Story, Nancy Wright (2) 134

Permissions Acknowledgments 137

Preface

I suppose it's taken me so gosh darn long to complete Smith & Kraus's 1999 scene and monologue books because it was a decade, a century, and indeed a millennium that I was reluctant to see come to an end. But come to an end it has, and here are the very best snippets I could find to help express a collective farewell to a magnificent decade of world theater while at the same time offering an enthusiastic greeting to a brand new age for our incredible dramatic journey.

Ladies, ladies, ladies. It's getting harder and harder to find cool stuff to satisfy your complex needs. What ever happened to the good old days when the greatest monologue moment for a woman was when she decided to leave a boring guy like Torvald, or when she just murdered her own sons and was waiting to be flown away from Thebes by the gods? Easy, easy stuff. Nowadays, actresses want and need more, and by golly, I've made it my sacred task in life to bring it to you.

What have I found for you this year, you may ask? I'll tell you: Those of you looking for stuff that will rock the director right out of his or her seat with it's manic intensity should look at *A.B.C. or The Man in the Red Suit* by Leslie Bramm, *Eve of Crimes: Memory Hotel* by Bob Jude Ferrante, *The Most Fabulous Story Ever Told* by Paul Rudnick, *The Connie Saxon Show* by Ethan Kanfer, *My Vicious Angel* by Christine Evans, *Alchemy* by Linda S. Wilkinson, *Bitch* by Elizabeth Ruiz and *When Will I Dance* by Claire Braz-Valentine.

If you'd like an opportunity to impress with your dramatic chops, definitely consider *Vernon Early* by Horton Foote, *Wash Out* by S. Heide Arbitter, *The Belles of the Mill* by Rachel Rubin Ladutke, *Blood Sky* by Yasmine Rana, *Blue Skies Forever* by Claire Braz-Valentine, *Eat the Breast* by Lindsay Price, *Never the Same Rhyme Twice* by Rooster Mitchell, *Officer Justice* by Janet Pound, *The Power of Love* by Sebastian Michael, *Moonshades* by

Wayne Paul Mattingly and *The Rim of the Wheel* by Daphne R. Hull.

Funnier (but not without a dramatic edge) ladies should look at *The Blueberry Café,* Women at Play by Ann Roth, *The "B" Word* by Dolores Whiskeyman, *Mercy Falls* by Jeni Mahoney, *What Corbin Knew* by Jeffrey Hatcher, *Zoë's Story* by Nancy Wright, *Are You All Right in There?* by David-Matthew Barnes and *The Serpent's Kiss* by me.

There's a lot of great material in this book, and I hope it was worth the wait . . . of course, you're sort of a captive audience, but what the heck, the 2000 books will be here before you know it.

Until then, I wish you all the best. Remember, if you find a monologue that you love, get a copy of the play and read every last word.

May you all suffer thousands upon thousands of broken legs!

Jocelyn Beard
The Brickhouse
Patterson, N.Y.

A.B.C. (or The Man in the Red Flannel Suit)

Leslie Bramm

Scene: A room in an old warehouse in Manhattan

Dramatic

B (48), ex-Marine and war hero. Texan. She sparks like a live wire.

> *B is a hired gun for an underground organization that plots revolution against the cloning of human beings. B has been sent to assassinate a clone on Thanksgiving Day. Here, she explodes with rage at the weak-willed society girl who has been assigned to be her partner.*

B: *Operation: Broken China.*

[A: A big nerve.]

B: I won the Silver Star, the Purple Heart and the Navy Cross! And when you address me you call me Sergeant!

[A: Yes M'am, Sergeant M'am.]

B: And don't call me M'am I work for a living.

> *(She takes a shot of scotch and opens the briefcase. The case is foamed lined and has the makings of a high-tech rifle inside. She begins to slowly assemble the weapon.)*

B: I love to kill! I mean, I fucking love to kill! A good kill is better than a good fuck. I'm talking about one of them slow, hard, fucks. A deep, biting, twisting, turning, ball slappin' you in the ass kinda fuck. A pulsating fuck that shoots through your body like a blue bolt. Kill, kill kill. Fuck, fuck, fuck, you starting to see my point?

> *(She pulls the bolt back exposing the weapon's chamber. She breathes in deeply and her body shudders.)*

B: Well hell. I've killed 'em standing up. Killed 'em lying down. Killed 'em when they least expected it. Killed 'em when they just stood there frozen in my sights. I even killed a man who was already dead once . . . Powder . . . Oil . . . Steel . . . Look how perfect it is. It's contour and balance . . . Look how perfectly it all fits. A hammer falls, a spark, an explosion, and a piece of steel is shot down a barrel. It collides with whatever it's pointed at . . . Every action happens without question. The powder doesn't question the spark. The spark doesn't challenge the trigger. The trigger in turn doesn't ask who the finger is that pulled it. There's no time for questions. No time for conscience. Hesitate and you're dead

A.B.C. (or The Man in the Red Flannel Suit)

Leslie Bramm

Scene: A room in an old warehouse in Manhattan

Dramatic

C (18), a slacker pizza delivery girl—brazen with smart-ass charm.

> *C has unknowingly stumbled upon two women who mean to kill her. When she discovers that one of them served in the Marines with her father, she shares the following dreadful secret.*

C: Can I tell you something? Something you can't tell anybody else?

[B: A secret, how covert.]

C: A big secret. You gotta promise.

[B: I'm a Marine.]

C: I need more scotch.

[B: It's that kind of a secret? Help yourself.]

    (C takes a long pull.)

[B: Hey take it easy.]

C: I don't care anymore.

[B: I do it's my scotch.]

    (She grabs the bottle away.)

C: I knew this kid. He played guitar. I thought he was cool. He was in a band. I let him fuck me once. What happens? . . . I mean, what could I do. I ain't ready for that. No fucking way . . . I hear about this guy. He's never been arrested. I knew somebody else that went to him. 3000 bucks right. He takes me into the back seat of his mustang. He does it right there in the car. It was foul. The smell, worse than this place. My pants come off. He doesn't wash his hands or nothing. Just

3

starts in on my twat with his dirty nails. He lights a joint, pops in a disk, and tells me; "Relax." He has this plastic, mustard, squeeze, bottle. That has liquid stuff in it. Shit brown and green stuff. It's supposed to numb me . . . It burned . . . Then it really fucking burns. I mean I may be part silicone but the shit was total agony. He says; "SHHH don't scream, 'cause if we get caught" . . . So there I am one leg over the front seat, one leg over this dude's shoulder, I'm staring at his greasy bald spot and chewing the collar off my leather jacket. He takes this long metal thing. I swear it's his dipstick. He starts scraping around inside of me. Scraping like he was looking for the last bit of mayo. And I'm thinking; "I could die right now." This guy was inches away from totally slaughtering me . . . Scraping and ripping and scraping and blood and scraping and blood and tearing and ripping, and vomit and me screaming inside my head. And the screaming gets louder and louder and it was like my head was going to bust . . . Then silence . . . Like being underwater . . . I didn't feel nothing . . . I realized I should have died the first time. When I hit the tree. I know it sounds messed up but I was meant to be dead.

(Beat.)

   I don't remember the rest. I fainted. In the cab ride home I could feel myself leaking all over the seat. But I survived. The ice packs, the infection, the scabs. I survived. The itching, the ointment, the clots of blood plopping out, having to piss in agony . . .

(Beat.)

[B: Why are you telling me this?]

C: 'Cause I'm drunk. I don't know. I mean . . . I don't know . . . You gotta tell somebody right?

The Adulterer

Jussi Wahlgren

Scene: Helsinki, Finland

Dramatic

Eva (55), a foul-mouthed elder scholar and shrewd politician at the University.

Eva's younger friend, Kris, is about to have an affair with a married professor. Here, Eva leaves a message on Kris's answering machine that contains uncanny insight into her friend's situation.

EVA: (*Enters the front of stage with a mobile.*) I was once accused of being too soft with a student when he had copied an assignment from somebody else. It happened in the early seventies. It was the Hippie time, flowers and peace and all that bull. He slept with me and I felt grateful. I never realized that I'm a woman and that men pay and pay all their lives for having a penis . . . It's true. I am the fucking female with the treasure and that's what they are after. Like my late husband. He cried when we did it for the first time. That's why I married him. He had feelings. He showed them. That's what I thought . . . What an asshole I was. When I'm gone, who cares who did what with whom and how many times. I'm just gone. It's a horrible thought. Nobody gives a shit. Maybe Robert Zyskovitz will remember one night when he's drunk at some fund-raising party that he fucked an assistant professor fifteen years ago. And now that woman is gone. Do you know what I mean, Kris? I know it sounds pathetic but, by God, that's what it is! I bet you're doing it right now. Is it Patrik or Phillip? Or the taxi driver. When I see you Kris, I see myself thirty years ago. Shit (*Cries slowly.*) . . . Sorry, I dropped the joint. It's not what you do but what other people think you're doing. Do you understand what I'm saying? You have to be a super human being to listen to your heart. I don't think it's even possible. I just don't believe in the "good" in man. I'm not saying that it's all so bad either, but . . . (*The call stops.*)

Alchemy

Linda Wilkinson

Scene: Here and now

Serio-comic
Anna (40s), lecturer in Physics at the university, currently ruminating about love.

Here, Anna shares a memory of a brief but passionate encounter with a sister academic.

ANNA: The first words I said to her were "I don't have a cat," what a stupid thing to say. All right if you are talking to another lesbian it's OK, kind of humorous. All lesbians have cats, but she wasn't a lesbian.

It was a few weeks ago at one of those interminable receptions at work. We were to welcome the new professor of Philosophy. The last one, Mogadon to his students, had expired in the middle of one of his lectures. Nobody had noticed for a while, well most of the room was asleep anyway.

So, I was standing, glass in hand (*Raises her glass.*) staring out of the window, dreaming of summer, and wondering when I could escape when I heard the hush, which meant he'd been ushered in. I say he, as even I had imagined that it would be a younger, male, version of Mogadon.

Was I wrong! (*Pause.*) However I stopped myself from spilling my wine I will never know. She wasn't beautiful, not in any conventional sense, but she had the bluest eyes and blackest hair I had ever seen. The boss was doing his introductions, "Dr. Elena Verdi, our new head of Philosophy and Psychology." When I thought about it later, I had heard of her. She's Italian and had been lecturing in Brno.

She smiled around the room, then our eyes met, (*Pause.*) I

couldn't look away and neither could she. In fact I don't think either of us even tried.

I watched from a distance wanting the swirling pit of desire in my stomach to die, but it wouldn't. He brought her nearer and nearer, introducing her to this one, that one, but whenever she could she stole a look in my direction. By the time it was my turn for introductions the wine was doing its worst. My mind had wandered past lust into eternity, "I don't have a cat." What could she answer?

"I do," she said, "a large fluffy Persian called Sophie." And she was gone, onto Gregor and his Art department.

Another glass of wine later she was standing before me. *(Bitterly.)* We should have done it then, in front of everybody else, we might just as well have done. Got it out of the way, over, finished.

We are about the same height, but I couldn't drag my eyes away from her breasts. She wore one of those girlie-type blouses, all soft fabric and pearl buttons.

I tried to focus on the conversation and ignore her cleavage. Tried not to imagine my fingers opening the buttons of her blouse until there was enough space for my hands to glide around the warm, soft, flesh, unhook her bra, take her nipple in my mouth and . . . *(Sighs.)*

"So, if you don't have a cat, what do you have?" she asked.

"I gave up on animals a while ago, they either die or leave you." I answered.

Looking into her face was no help. Her eyes pulled me toward them. I felt as if I were melting, dissolving. She wanted me too.

"Yes, animals and people both. That is what you meant?" She teases and talked a bit about the philosophy of attachment, to animals, *(Heavily ironic.)* and I about the theory of Chaos and how our fields weren't so dissimilar really; how small variations in life can make a highly ordered state, whether it be a mind or the Universe, spiral out of control.

And all the time I knew that she was trouble. She wasn't

8

afraid of what was happening between us. All around I could feel the "Poor old sad sick lesbian stance" being directed toward me, but she didn't care.

She sipped her wine and looked me straight in the eye. I looked at the engagement ring on her finger, she blushed and told me about *her man*; but the desire was still there; I wasn't the only one imagining what it would be like between us with no clothes, a bed and a long, long weekend.

The next day, after I sobered up, I decided to give her a miss. It, she, wasn't worth it, I'd been there with straight women too many times. I didn't want a loving friend, I wanted . . . oh, I don't know any more.

So I played polite in the coffee room and made sure we were never there alone, but one day she caught me out.

"Have I done anything?"

"They'll think you're like me." I said.

"Let them."

Let them, easily said. I still went on avoiding her.

I swam and ran and looked forward to the summer. Last week she left a ticket in my pigeon hole. It was for a student performance, *The Man In Love with Death,* a play about Michel Foucault. Not the most uplifting of titles you would agree, but then she is a philosopher. It was very strange, the whole play consisted of a bald man, clothed in black, who sat in a chair, facing a mirror, posing himself questions which he never answered.

After the performance she asked me back to her flat; for a bite to eat. I know, I know I shouldn't have gone, but I did. (*Pause.*) We walked through one of those light spring showers, which appear out of nowhere and end just as quick; (*Pain and sarcasm mixed together.*) a bit like what happened between us really. (*Stands and runs her hands through her hair.*)

She cooked, and I sat on the floor talking and watching the breeze ruffle the curtains. We ate pasta or something, the food was immaterial. The word *friend* resonated through my brain louder and louder, could I do it, should I? Could I tread on my desire so completely that we became good old-fashioned "girlfriends"? Because she wasn't getting any more than that. (*Laughs with self mocking irony.*)

"You're quiet," she said "what are you thinking?"

I should have talked about friendship, but my mind had moved beyond that, "I suppose you want me to make love to you?" I said, "like all the others have, all the other nice straight women looking for a thrill."

She blushed and sipped her wine, silence hung like a lead weight.

"I can't say no," she finally said, laughing almost to herself, "I can't say no."

Neither could I, but this time I wasn't going to be the seducer, she had to really want me. Not just be curious, not be looking for a bit of titillation, she had to want the whole naked, orgasmic package.

(*She stands facing the audience, recalling what happened, she is becoming emotional and angry, but also full of sadness. At first, her hands are clenched by her sides, then she begins slowly undoing the buttons on her shirt beneath which she wears a camisole. Holds her arms aloft and turns slowly. Stops when facing the audience throws her head back then runs her hands down her body, over her breasts and down to her pubis, then focuses once more on the audience, but she is still in the room in her head.*)

She took me, (*Sighs.*) how she took me. When I was completely naked she looked at me long and hard, it was impossible to decipher what was going through her mind. Finally she stood and began to peel away her own clothes. Her skin glowed amber and gold in the twilight. I knew that she would taste, and smell, of the earth sweet, rich and tangy. Smiling she came toward me, her hard dark nipples brushed against mine, warm and wanting; (*Pause.*) and then she kissed me. For a long moment, that was all, we stood immobile with our arms and tongues entwined.

Then suddenly, her lips, her tongue, were everywhere and we were on the floor . . . (*Pause.*)

The room exploded into a thousand pieces I, . . . I. There was no fear in the way she loved me, no fear in the way she buried her head between my legs (*Holds her pubis.*) and took me over the edge of passion into a place I had never imagined before, I felt my skin dissolve, I pulsated at her every touch, there were no boundaries any more, (*Pause.*) for either of us. (*Pause.*) I have never been so free. (*Pause.*) Evening became night, and night became dawn, at some point we had ceased to be separate entities, or even human. It was all color, light, and sensation. Her body was . . . (*Lost in thought.*) . . . I don't want to remember . . . I thought I wanted revenge for all those past encounters yet, even though I knew what would happen afterwards . . . (*Pause.*) when the sunrise burst red and gold over us I was making love to her as tenderly and deeply as I could. She vibrated beneath my touch and opened herself to me completely without inhibition or question, (*Pause then very softly.*) she was so beautiful.

(*Pause, she is near to tears.*)

It was long past dawn when I left. She smiled up at me from the bed which we had shared for the last hours of the night and said nothing. On the way home I realized that we hadn't spoken at all, not once. She said some word to herself, over and over when I . . . , we were . . . oh shit. (*Shakes her head and comes back to consciousness. Looks down and starts buttoning her shirt. Sits down and takes another slug of wine. Before speaking bitterly.*) She never showed up for work that day.

Are You All Right in There?

David-Matthew Barnes

Scene: A bathroom

Serio-comic

Gina (17), a high school student musing about her life in small-town America.

> *Gina locks herself in the bathroom during a party and takes a few moments to contemplate her past, present, and future.*

GINA: I'm sorry. (*Pauses.*) I am sorry. I'm just kind of emotional right now. (*Pauses.*) I think it's graduation. I'm graduating in a month and I can't wait to get out of here. (*Pause.*) My hometown. My friends. My family. (*Pause.*) I hate these people. And I feel so . . . guilty for it. I must be the most horrible person in the entire world. I hate this party. I hate Jimmy Foster for inviting me in the first place. I hate my best friend. I hate my boyfriend. (*Pause.*) But I really hate Brittany Tyler. She's evil and she has a bad haircut. (*Pause.*) I am so horrible. Something is seriously wrong with me. I have lived here for all of my life. I should be proud of where I come from. I should look back with fond memories and kind thoughts—but I just can't wait to leave. (*Pauses.*) I don't know why. I really don't. It's like this . . . feeling. I wake up in the morning and it just chokes me. It's the same house and the same people and the same school—I just can't take it anymore. I am only seventeen. I should be happy. I should be sweet. I should do a lot of charity work in the community. (*Panics.*) What if I'm nuts? What if I need serious help—like therapy or something medieval like that? My aunt went to therapy for six months and she totally gained thirty pounds. She blew up like a house. Then she almost choked to death one night. She was lying in bed—eating a box of Crunch 'N' Munch—and she was watching this really sad movie and she started to cry—and I guess one of those little popcorn kernels got stuck in her throat or something—anyway, she almost died. But she's okay now—I guess. She sells Tupperware and she's dating this guy named Bob. He used to live on a commune and he refuses to take a shower. It's a really sick relationship—if you ask me. (*Pauses.*) This party is pathetic. I could be at home right now, curled up in bed and reading *Wuthering Heights.* Instead—I was standing in the living room and this foreign-exchange student kept staring with this weird look on his face. He comes up to me and says (*Imitates accent.*) "Oh, you are such a beautiful American girl!" So I looked at him—at the top of his pointy little head because he was shorter than my patience —and I told him that he smelled. Because he did. Like cat puke or something gross like that. So he started yelling at me in his native language and it freaked me out. I thought he was psychotic. Then he walked away as if it were supposed to shatter my heart into a million tiny pieces. (*Pauses.*) Puh-leaze, Don Juan— either go home or grow. So he slithered his way around the room until he found Leslie. She's . . . real. She thinks she's cool because she went to Paris last summer and made out with some French guy at the Eiffel Tower. I'll tell you how I really feel about Leslie. She has the personality of a cheese grater. She's been a cheerleader since she was in diapers and she thinks we should worship her because she knows how to jump in the air and do a cartwheel. Trust me—I have been to a football game and I have seen the girl dance. It's not pretty. She should consider buying herself a little bit of rhythm before she goes to college. (*Pause.*) You know—this whole party was Madeline's idea—as usual. She's my best friend - and I hate her guts. I don't want to sound really negative or anything, but I had this dream—that I killed her . . . in a swimming pool. I held her head down in the water until—never mind. (*Pauses.*) I don't want to think about it. It will give me nightmares. Anyway, she does this all the time—Madeline—she'll get all excited about some party we're invited to. She'll spend four hundred hours picking out the right sleazy outfit to wear. Then, we'll drive to the party together in her Dad's new car and we'll walk in together. And then no less than five minutes after we've arrived—she is gone. Nowhere in sight. Disappeared. I don't know where she goes for hours—but I have a feeling that it looks like a *(Breaks the word up.)* bed—room. Oh, I am not insinuating that she has sex *(Pauses.)* I know she does. In fact, the whole town knows it. I'm embarrassed for her really. *(Pauses.)* Maybe I'm her friend because I feel sorry for her. See, her family is kind of messed up—but then again, whose isn't? I mean—my Mom and I—we get along great. *(Pauses.)* Really. Really, we do. I swear. *(Pauses.)* Do you believe me? *(Pauses.)* Yeah, me neither. *(Looks around the bathroom, at the décor.)* This house is so *tacky*. The Fosters are really strange people. They buy polyester clothes and they wear straw hats and put rhinestone collars on their poo-dle—believe me, I hate that dog. Their son Jimmy the stud—he has parties here all the time because his parents love to travel so much. You should meet these people. They are frightening. Then again, this whole town is demented and disturbed. I don't know how I ended up here. I just can't wait to get out. *(Places a hand over her stomach.)* My stomach keeps growling. I really want a taco. The food here completely sucks. *(Pauses.)* There I go again —being negative. *(Madeline enters the hallway and stands just outside of the bathroom door. Madeline is dressed to give credi-bility to her reputation. A purse hangs from her bare shoulder. She gazes over a shelf of porcelain music boxes, against the wall in the hallway. Madeline puts her ear to the door, straining to hear Gina, still eyeing the music boxes.)* You know—I think I want to be on *The Young and The Restless* someday. Then, life would be good.

Bad Buddhists

Robert Vivian

Scene: A run-down sleeping room in the dark, withering interior of a major mid-western city

Dramatic

Petey (22), a young women trying to escape from life's encroaching emptiness.

> Petey has encountered Grossman while walking the streets at night and accompanied him back to the place where he sleeps. Here, the lonely young women reveals the sadness that threatens to overwhelm her at any moment.

PETEY: And I . . . and I . . . am just sitting here, knowing that no one sees me for me. No one cares. No one listens.

[GROSSMAN: It's a bitch all right.]

PETEY: I'm not used to people talking about their fears and wishes. It's like a door's been thrown open. (*Pause.*) You know, there's so much I don't believe in. It's hard to get up in the morning sometimes. I work at a dentist's office as an assistant. I stare into people's mouths all day. Sometimes you see the most incredible rainbows. (*Pause.*) I always think of donkeys for some reason. And it's hard not to pity these mouths. And my deep, dark secret is that there's not enough pity in the world. There's just not enough. (*Pause.*) Going home the other day, I stopped off to mail a bill. This old woman was working the cash register. She was training for the job! I wanted to stop everything and hug her right there. This other young lady was telling her what to do. Outside it was cold and windy. I wanted to buy a sweater. A gray sweater. I wanted to give it to the old lady. I wanted to hold her in my arms. There's no justice. We just live on, doing the best we can. There's no satisfying beginning or end.

The Belles of the Mill

Rachel Rubin Ladutke

Scene: Congressional Hearings, Washington, D.C., March 2,1912

Dramatic
Bridget Gallagher (18), an Irish mill worker, strong-willed and courageous.

> *When Bridget is beaten by the police during a mill worker's*
> *strike in Lawrence, Massachusetts, she is subsequently*
> *recruited by the union to address Congress on behalf of the*
> *women who suffer and die in the mills.*

BRIDGET: Representative Berger and members of the Committee.
I am Bridget Eileen Gallagher, from Ireland. I am eighteen years
old. When I was fifteen, my mother took me to Cork and put me
on a boat to America. She told me there was nothing for me in
Ireland. And she was right. I was so excited to be going to
America. Terrified too, o' course. When I first got off the boat, I
felt like I was in a different world from everyone and every place
I'd ever known and loved. I've never felt so alone in my life. And
I was right to be scared. I don't mind hard work, but there's a
great difference between hard work and slavery.

   You all may think, you may have been told, that this strike is
just a group of troublemakers who want to destroy the city. But
it's not true. The strikers I've met have as much of a stake in
Lawrence as the mill officials and politicians do. More, even.
We're the ones that live there, and shop there, and worship
there. Meanwhile, not a single one of the mill officials, from second hand on up, live in Lawrence if they can afford not to.

   Do you know what it's like inside a mill? Have you ever had
to set foot in one of those hellholes? Day after day, I can hardly
get the sound out of my ears. Thread flying through the air.
Thread working its way into my lungs. I once saw an older

women—she must have had years of experience—get her dress caught in the machinery. I rushed to turn it off, but it was too late. She died right there, on the floor. They came and carried her out, and the boss told us just to keep working like nothing had happened. And we did. We were afraid of losing our jobs if we stopped for five minutes.

Another time, I saw a young girl—younger than me, maybe fourteen—got her hair pulled into the machine. It practically pulled her whole body in. She was scalped. She was in the hospital seven months, and as soon as she got out, she went to work in a different mill. I was working right next to her that day. It could just as easily have been me. You get tired, and the machines go faster and faster, and there's no chance of a break. If we want fresh water, we have to pay ten cents a week for it. And then 'tisn't even cold, or fresh. Ever since I came to Lawrence I've worked six days a week in the mill. Death is all around me, death and pain and suffering, it has been since I first came to Lawrence, and I see no end to it.

I love this country for what I've always known it could be. But working in the mills kills your hopes and dreams, and even your spirit. Do you love this country as much as I do? Aye, of course you do. You must. Nobody could live here and not realize what an amazing, wonderful place it is. You must see that strike had to happen, and that something has got to change. We've done what we can. Now it's up to you.

Bitch

Elizabeth Ruiz

Serio-comic

Zocorro (mid 30s), a jewelry designer who makes a living delivering marijuana on a bicycle. Jamaican and Mexican decent. Culturally on the fringe.

When the betraying Fran returns to town, Zocorro takes a minute to remind her friend, Sara, why she shouldn't let Fran stay with her.

ZOCORRO: Don't do this, Sara. She royally screwed you.

[SARA: How?]

ZOCORRO: *How?* How can you say "How?"

[SARA: I'm beginning to think it was all so petty.]

ZOCORRO: Yes. *She* was petty and very hurtful.

[SARA: Remind me. Tell me everything she did to me. Whatever you can remember. 'Cause I feel like I'm losin' perspective. I'm so . . . tired.]

ZOCORRO: Okay. I'll start at the beginning. As I recall, you started off as romantic rivals in high school.

[SARA: You're gonna go that far back?]

ZOCORRO: *Until* one day in the girl's room, she confronted you and declared that you shouldn't think she'd stolen your guy, 'cause he had thousands of girlfriends, besides the two of you. This, of course, impressed you. So, she persuaded you into a revenge plan against your mutual, cheatin' boyfriend and one of the other rivals. You became fast friends, but then, after you had vowed to abstain from Raul . . . that was his name right? . . . and seek retribution only . . .

[SARA: I can't believe you remember these details.]

ZOCORRO: . . . She went off alone with him at a party and gave him a blow job which she later described to you in detail, and which you later described to me in detail. *That* I would never forget, given that I was a straight-laced, savin'-it-for-my-husband type back then and got my jollies through you, though I pretended to be shocked. You, as I recall, did not want to appear "uncool" and hid your jealousy and hurt feelings. After all, so-called casual sex could not be held against a "sister" in those days. Then, about a year and a half past the Raul stage, she invited your new boyfriend, Mike, to visit an aunt in Asbury Park for the weekend, knowing that your father was in hospital and that you couldn't go. A year later you found out they'd slept together that weekend, but by then you'd started seeing a new guy, and decided to let bygones by. Should I go on?

[SARA: Please.]

ZOCORRO: Fran always had to be the center of everyone's life, so she made friends with your cousin, Deirdre, and then gossiped maliciously between the two of you. Always conniving. Always causing misunderstandings, until she managed to break the two of you apart. To this day you're estranged from your Deirdre. She ruined your friendship with several people, gossiped about your sex life to your own mother. And let's not forget how she let you down when your father was dying. Or how she kicked your brother out on the street when he needed a place to crash because her new, Mexican boyfriend . . .

[SARA: Whom she married . . .]

ZOCORRO: . . . was jealous of your brother. You defended your brother, and Fran decided to move out with only a coupl'a days' notice, bad-mouthing you to the landlord so he refused to give you a new lease. That's what I recall about your "sister soul" as the two of you used to call each other. (*Beat.*) Although, she was always nice to me. Am I leaving anything out?

BITCH
Elizabeth Ruiz

Dramatic
Sara (mid 30s), a theater-artist of working-class Hispanic origins, culturally on the fringe.

> *Rough times have forced Sara to take in a roommate—the younger, idealistic Annie. When Annie discovers Sara's pet lizard while snooping, things get a little tense.*

SARA: I thought you wanted to know me!

[ANNIE: That's okay, Sara, I'm sorry if I pressured you. I don't need to know . . .]

SARA: (*She releases Annie's collar, but stalks her, holding the lizard menacingly.*) Yes! Yes! You need to know. (*Cornering her up against the wall.*) I had a shitty fucking childhood okay! Do you think you might have guessed that? The details don't matter, although I know that that's what you want, right? You want to steal the details of my life to fill in the empty holes in your stingy, repressed little existence, but trust me, they don't matter. The details don't matter. All you need are the generalizations. I'm broke. Do you think you might have guessed that? Huh? I know you found my unemployment check!

(*Annie tries to move away. Sara holds her against the wall with one hand.*)

[ANNIE: That was an accident, it got mixed up with my mail . . .]

SARA: I've worked hard all my life and I have nothing to show for it. And like most women past thirty who did not go the Betty Crocker route, I've been lied to and deceived by men! Why? You might ask. "Why?" Because I DARED to survive without them. I really don't fuckin' know! I just don't get this "love" shit, quite frankly. And yes! I just broke up with one of the delicate little fuckin' flowers, in case you're dying to know!

But I have found that women are equally as deceitful and undependable. And I wonder where I could get such an idea! (*Pause.*) What else do you wanna know? Did I love my Daddy? YES! YES I LOVED THE FUCKIN' SON OF A BITCH. And my fuckin' mommy? Yes! I love my fuckin' mommy. Every time she brings me chicken soup when I have the fuckin' flu I get down on my knees and praise the Lord! Okay? Are you happy now?
(*Annie is terrified.*)

Let's go over it again. I had a lousy childhood. I'm unemployed. I just broke up with a man, and I love mommy and daddy. Okay? Have you got that? I said have you got that?
(*Annie nods.*)

Good. And as far as you're concerned, I know everything there is to know about you, too. You're from Boston. You're Greek on your father's side. You have a lot of adolescent fantasies about the life of theatricals in the Big City, weighed down by trendy ideas about the art scene, and you're a goddamned trust fund baby, born mid-way into Generation X. I was born on the late side of the Baby Boomers, in case you were dying to know.

[ANNIE: (*Trembling.*) Don't they call that the Lost Generation?]

SARA: No, they don't. Don't they teach you anything in those Ivy League schools? Now stay out of my things and stay the fuck away from my goddamned lizard!

Blood Sky

Yasmine Rana

Scene: A rural roadside

Dramatic

Joley (30), a women trying to make sense of her troubled past.

Here, Joley remembers a night shortly after she left home when violence came close to claiming her soul.

JOLEY: (*To audience.*) We were driving down this dark road leading to nowhere one night. Me and this guy . . . boy . . . person . . . whatever, I met somewhere along the way. It was the summer I left home. And it was a night just like this one. Steaming hot. You know, the kind of hot that overtakes your whole body. It's the kind of hot you experienced as a child when you were sick with a fever, and you would just lie still, and stare into the dark, and listen to the stillness pounding so hard into your head that it almost made you mad. Remember how you couldn't escape from that stillness? Every creak and tear sounded like a never ending piercing scream. Well that's how that night was. With me and this . . . guy. Music up. Windows down. Dust left behind. Tire tracks pressed hard into the ground. He was driving so fast. And I looked out of my window, into the sky. And the sky was blood red. I swear to you. I had never seen anything like that before. It was like the sky was leading us to the middle of nowhere. It wasn't taking us to Hell. Hell would have been easier to define. It wouldn't have been so frightening because it's something you understand. Hell's a concept you were taught as a child. It was a hanging threat drilled into your head by some traveling preacher in some dust-filled church hall in that little town you spent seventeen years trying to escape from. You would know what to expect from Hell. It would be bad, but not surprisingly bad. You wouldn't have to worry. Your expectations would most definitely be met. You know hell. But this . . . sky . . . place wasn't Hell. It was more terrifying. Unknown. No-man's-land. A wasteland. I don't really remember where exactly we were coming from, or what we had done before. It doesn't matter. But I don't know why the sky was like that. I remember I was looking for some break. Some blue or black or gray. But there was no relief, just blood everywhere. And this sky overwhelmed my mind and body in such a way that I asked him to stop the car. I told him we had to. I thought and truly felt the whole world was on fire, and it would soon catch up with us. No matter how fast or far we drove, this "blood sky" would find us. It would know our where-abouts, where we were coming from, where we were going. It would always be there, waiting for us to get tired of running, and therefore, give up. It would win. He laughed and told me I was crazy. This guy wanted me to explain. I couldn't put it into words. It's just that I felt something so horrible, so treacherous. You know when something is so bad you can't explain it. You can't even say it out loud because you're afraid once it's said, it'll happen.

The Blueberry Café
Women at Play
Katherine Burkman, Jane Cottrell, Martha Lovely, Cecily O'Neill,
Ann Roth, Cathy Ryan, Linda Sheppard, Lindsey Alexander Stout
and Christine Warner. The following excerpts written by Ann Roth.

Scene: A café

Serio-comic
Susie (20s–30s), a women who knows a thing or two about dogs.

> *When Susie runs into an old flame, she is incensed to discover that he barely remembers her.*

SUSIE: Joe? Is that you? Do you remember me? (*Laughs nervously.*) It's really strange, I mean it's been how long? What is it? fifteen years, twenty years? Oh what am I thinking? Of course you don't remember. Oh you do not. You know you don't, Joe. (*Looking around.*) Isn't this Café wonderful.
> *(Waitress comes over. Chorus of those on stage hum a bit of Blueberry Café song.)*

Yes I'd love something, a glass of Pinot. (*To audience.*) Is this weird? He doesn't remember at all. I know that. They never do, but I'm going to have fun because I do remember it all! I just can't resist. He looks very good, gray beard, body still nice.
> *(Waitress brings drink.)*

Thanks. So here we are. (*Toasts him.*) So do you? Do you remember me? Are you at least trying to place me? You can't, can you? Oh I know you can't Joe. I can tell—those eyes can't lie. Well maybe a little. Still iridescent blue. (*Pause for deep breath.*) OK Joe. Twenty years ago this summer. I'll give you just the smallest of hints. We'll start with Jerry and Irene. They designated you to pick up Irene's sister Martha and me, our first weekend of living in Manhattan. You remember? OK, so where did you pick us up? No, wrong Joe, not Gramercy Park. The Village. Bleeker and East Broadway. Yes, in that little yellow Alpha. Yah, sure, you remember that car. Your all-time favorite car. Stop laughing Joe. *(Determined.)* Now concentrate. When we arrived at Jerry and Irene's, 86th and Riverside Dr., what was happening, yeah happening. Where did I stand most of the time? No, not in the kitchen. At the window, Joe. I stood looking out at the river and New Jersey. It was all so glorious and it was all mine. You were watching me—I could feel it—then what? You and I went over to a little Broadway deli to pick up dinner for everyone. I couldn't think of much to say so I just laughed at you a lot. You were real funny then. *(She takes a large drink and continues.)* OK Joe, let the masochism continue. Oh sure Joe, pour me another glass. *(Takes a drink.)* Just what I need. So after dinner, Joe? What happened? No, you didn't take us home. You took ME and left Martha with Steve and Irene. So, what did we do? Sure pour me another. I'm drinking fast. *(To audience.)* Mmm, that's what I did then. *(To Joe.)* So Joe just tell me. Did you come into my apartment? Oh, don't even try to answer that—you don't even remember. Well, did you come in? A lot went on, a LOT. Then I said NO and pushed you away. Yea, you're right, "girls from Ohio," that's us. You did ask me to go with you the next day. Amazing. Where, Joe, did you ask me to go? No, not the Bronx Zoo. Coney Island, and I hated amusement parks, especially the hideous rides. Now what ride did you take me on? The Parachute Jump? Oh, for God's sake Joe, the Roller Coaster. It was terrifying and you held me very tight. *(Laughs.)* You have a dog? Well, that's great. I'm a dog person. Named Yoda? I see. Nice name. Star Wars, huh? He's your comfort and confidante? You prefer him to most people? I'm sure you do. He's easy and never forgets? Ha, ha, so am I. Yoda doesn't have the same expectations. Oh Joe, don't worry your gray little head. You've had two failed relationships? What do you expect me to say? We've all had our sorrows; I mean, after all, it's been twenty years. *(Looks out imaginary window.)* Look, there's a gorgeous full moon. For heaven's sake, Joe, you don't have to be so literal. So, it's afternoon. You do remember the moon, don't you Joe? It seems most everyone has forgotten her. Mars has taken her place. Much more interesting geologically they say. (*Gets up and goes to imaginary window.*) But, hey, I haven't forgotten.

The Blueberry Café

Women at Play

Katherine Burkman, Jane Cottrell, Martha Lovely, Cecily O'Neill, Ann Roth, Cathy Ryan, Linda Sheppard, Lindsey Alexander Stout and Christine Warner. The following excerpts written by Ann Roth.

Scene: A café

Serio-comic

Alissa (15–17), a young girl whose mother has fixed her up on a blind date.

> *Alissa is furious that her mom has fixed her up with a geek and here expresses her ire in full-blown teen angst.*

ALISSA: (*In a rage, confronting an audience member as her mother.*) I'm not going back down those stairs, Mom. I'm not. I won't, I can't. Don't make me, please, please, please. Because he's horrible, ugly, horrible, disgusting, that's why. Well, of course his mother didn't tell you that! He has on a bow tie. Oh, God, and white shoes. A bow tie and white shoes. Never, never, never, I'm not budging from this room! (*Pause.*) Yes I just left him there. I don't know, I guess he's talking to him . . . well, I'm not worried about what Daddy will say . . . What do you mean, how could I do it? I opened the door, took one long look and said excuse me, I've got to get something. Ran upstairs and here I stay. You have to go downstairs and get rid of him, yes you do. No, no, no, I will not budge, stop it, you're not strong enough to drag me. Stop it, that hurts! Now go, will you? . . . You're laughing. Oh my God, how can you laugh? What? You think Dad is telling those boring football stories to him? The galloping ghost and the flying tackles with no padding. (*Starting to giggle, despite herself.*) How could he? That nerd wouldn't know a football from a hockey puck. (*Laughing.*) Now stop it, mom, this is not funny. (*Trying to control herself and getting more agitated.)* Stop laughing, will you, and go downstairs, please. I don't know, tell him anything. Tell him I was stricken, yes stricken, very ill. I am stricken, Mom. My stomach turned over when I opened the front door. What do you mean I can't do this? I'm doing it. I don't care if it's only one evening. No, I will not meet someone else when I'm with him! No one would even consider that? What? What are you giggling about? Stop that. This is terrible for me and you're laughing. Yes, he does really have on white shoes and a bow tie. *(Starts giggling again despite herself.)* Whose Harry Franklin? He what? He wore bow ties and white shoes? You were crazy about him? *(Trying to stop laughing.)* That was a hundred years ago, Mom. Now stop it. What do you mean, poor Dad? I'm sure he's doing just dandy. What does he care—t's not his blind date. If you're so worried get down there and tell him I'm sick. Please, you can do it, Mom. *(Very agitated.)* I'm not going! Please, please, please. No, I don't care how embarrassing it is. So you play bridge with his mother. So what. What about me? NOW DO IT. You won't hurt his feelings. Just lie and say good-bye. For me, Mom. Oh God, please, please. I won't move from this spot, I can promise you that. You can't make me. Just go, go, go!

> *(She has covered her face and is sobbing. She peers out behind her hands and sees her mom leaving the room.)*

Oh, thank you lord. Go, go, hurry, yes, yes, yes. She's down there. I can hear her little voice. Now close the door. Do it. Yes. Done. *(Pause. Sees Mom.)* He's really gone? See, you did it. Thank God! Oh, no Mom, I didn't mean that . . . right . . . right. God wouldn't lie, but he also wouldn't have fixed me up with that geek. OK? *(Sheepishly.)* Did he believe you? Oh no, you gave him what? The leftover meat loaf and a box of candy? *(Starts to giggle through tears, then laugher.)* The leftover meat loaf and a box of candy! The leftover meat loaf and a box of candy! Mom, Mom, stop it. You're making me laugh, now stop it . . . it's not funny . . . No, it isn't.

Blue Skies Forever

Claire Braz-Valentine

Scene: July 1937

Dramatic

Amy Earhart (70s), Amelia Earhart's mother.

Following her famous daughter's disappearance, Amy does her best to cope with the fact that she might never return.

AMY: Amelia loved her country more than most. And, if some day someone proves that she might have done something on the flight for her country, something that endangered her, that caused this awful end, then so be it. She would have been proud to go that way. And I would be proud of her too. It's so very hard to accept that she's gone. It's as if any minute that phone is going to ring, and it will be her, and she will have landed somewhere, and she'll be fine. (*She gets up, goes to sideboard.*) I really need to make things ready in case that happens. For when she calls. She'll need things. (*She picks up suitcase and puts it on the table.*) I'm going to have things ready for her. She's very fussy, you know, about cleanliness. She likes things just so. A mother knows these things. She'll need clean underwear, (*Packs underwear.*) and a clean blouse, (*Packs clean blouse.*) and a nice skirt, and a sweater, a brown one. (*Holds sweater up to her face and begins crying.*) And a comb and scissors for that hair of hers. She hates it when her hair gets too long. Never can control that silly hair. I'll cut it for her before we allow any photographs. Then she'll be pretty again. Then it will be fine again. Everything back to normal. And you can interview her. It's a shame you never met her. I know you'll like her. Everyone likes her. (*She closes suitcase and sets it down beside her chair and sits again.*) There, that's ready. I must keep this close by. All the time. Amelia would expect it of me, to be there for her. I won't let her down. I'll be there for her when she needs me. What's a mother for, if she can't be there for her children? My mind is wandering again. It's been so very difficult. (*Changes of mood. Breaking down.*) Landa Goshen, what am I going to do without her? Why, she'd just call and take me flying at the drop of a hat, just like that! Oh how I loved that. (*Cries.*) We'd go on for hours. My girl and me. I'd just sit right there next to her in the cockpit, let her fly in peace, and I'd just read a book and look out the window. Look down at the towns, watching the sea turn golden in the sunset. And the trees! Amelia said no one ever saw a tree until they saw one from the sky, and the shadow it made on the land. She said trees are so much more beautiful from the top, the way God sees them. (*Sobs.*) Oh Amelia. My little girl. I'm not ready for this. (*Pulls herself together with great effort.*) You know, Amelia wrote poetry from the time she was a little girl. Out of everything she ever wrote I have a favorite. I say it over and over to myself these days. It comforts me.

Courage is the price that life exacts for granting peace.
The soul that knows it not, knows no release.
From little things.
Knows not the livid loneliness of fear,
Nor mountain heights,
where bitter joy can hear
The sound of wings.
(*Closes scrapbooks. Looks at audience, smiles.*)
Good girl Amelia. Good girl.

Blue Skies Forever

Claire Braz-Valentine

Scene: July 1937

Dramatic
Amelia Earhart (30s)

Here, the famous aviator explains her life and her love: flying.

AMELIA: When I'm in the air, away from . . . this earth, when I'm not land-bound, it's like I've gone through a window . . . a portal of reality, and then out the other side . . . and I'm floating along the seam of the universe, and I am free in the solitude of centuries. And no one knows my name, my gender.

When I am in that space between heaven and earth, where so few women have been, people don't know what to make of me. They call me a loner. They say I'm different, difficult to understand, cool, aloof, withdrawn, preoccupied. Of course they are right. I'm worse than that. I am a dangerous woman. I am a determined woman. I am not normal. I live for life at the edge . . . where nothing stagnates, nothing's the same. I walk that high wire into the great adventure. And I love every minute of it. This is what I've always wanted. And I have no patience waiting for the times to change . . . to catch up with me. They will never catch up.

When I am in the air . . . I am where I belong . . . in that place where nothing stands still, everything moves, and it's never boring. Everything is always new. It's always the first time in the theater of angels, of birds . . . the kingdom of wings. My body feels heavy on land. My bones are solid.

When I am up there soaring . . . through the fingers of God, with my hand on the throttle, I am beyond woman or man, above gender, and the lust of earthly sex, the longings of simple skin. When I am up there in the beautiful blindness of clouds, I am above it all . . . of having to fit in, of being accepted and desired, of being what's expected. I am the unexpected, the unforeseen. I am your astonishment. I am on the other side. Where no one judges you by the shape of your body, length of your hair, color of your skin, the lines on your face, or the cut of your clothes. I am released. Free.

I don't want to land. I want more space. I don't want to land.

I always expected everything, and I ignored the rules against women. The roles against women. I was not born to follow rules or to play a role, for anyone. I was born to search, to push, to try something new, to let other women know they must not be caged. To give them freedom. To tell them they are not play-things, but players. It's all there for them. The only price they pay to get it is courage. Once you have courage the doors are open. And you go through them. And once you go through these doors, you are in the company of daring women, dangerous women, dear women who will inspire you, challenge you, lead you to the horizons of your dreams.

Honor knows no gender. Courage knows no gender.

I have stood before hundreds of thousands and said these words and it was written that I wore a blue dress with matching necklace, that I was gracious, almost lovely, thoroughly feminine, not like a boy at all. I have flown beside my courageous sisters who have crashed and died in the pursuit to their independence and their dreams, and it is called a Power Puff Derby, the Sweethearts of the Air. We are not America's sweethearts. And, no, we are not like boys, at all.

I have paid my dues to become this woman.

I married my promoter who raised the money to pay for my plane.

I will use it to leave him.

I will use it to leave everyone,

even myself.

I did not love him nor his earthbound sex,

but I would have spread my legs for the devil

so I could spread my wings.

They call my plane Electra,
Electra who longed for her father
I long for no man . . . I long for the air.
I yearn for freedom at any price.
At the ultimate price.
I lift
I thrust
I pitch
I roll
I spin
I glide above you
I am
Airborne
out of your reach
away from your eyes
closer to God.
Forever.
The sky is my lover, my destiny.
They call me Lady Lindy,
But I am no lady.
My name is Amelia,
and I am
A Flier.

The "B" Word

Dolores Whiskeyman

Scene: Here and now

Serio-comic

Edna (30s), a woman who's had a bad day.

Here, exasperated Edna weaves a dark tale of road rage run amok and retribution denied by fate.

EDNA: I know, I'm late. And I'm not going to give you any excuses. But I do have a reason. If you want to hear it. *(Beat.)* See. It happened again. This morning. Some guy in traffic cuts me off—and takes offense that I take offense. I give him this. *(Shakes her fist.)* and he gives me this *(Obscene gesture.)* Then he yells: B——!!! *(Covering her mouth.)*

You know: That Word. The B Word.

Okay. You've heard it before, I've heard it before. Used it before—it's not like I'm an innocent, burning ears, all that. It's just that when it's aimed at YOU—with the full force of a howitzer about to go off in your face—it takes on a new kind of meaning. You see it in print, it's just another word, right? Like the 10,000 or so other words in my unabridged Random House dictionary.

(She throws the dictionary down on the desk for emphasis.)

Look: Right here it is: The B word means, and I quote: a female dog. A female of canines generally. Chihuahua, Pekinese, Wolfhound, Fox? Okay. Fine. B-word, dog, dog, b-word. Rather clinical, fine. You DOG! YOU CUT ME OFF IN TRAFFIC! But I read on: slang. A malicious, unpleasant, selfish women, especially one who stops at NOTHING to reach her goal. AH HA! There it is! Ambition. AMBITION is what distinguishes the sweet-natured paragon of goodness otherwise known as woman from the harpy we call a BITCH!

(Slaps her hand over her mouth.)

There, I said it. Bitch. Root word of AMBITION. Am—bitch—on.

Am—BITCH—on. I want, therefore I do. And get the hell out of my way.

So then I think. You know. Bitch is just a word. Say it fast, it loses its power. Like Rutabaga. Think about it. Roooooot-a-bay-ga. (*Quickly.*) Rutabaga, Rutabaga, rutabaga, rutabaga, rutabaga, rutabaga, rutabaga—it stops being a strange vegetable and becomes a collection of sounds with no real impact. It's just noise. Like the B word—and all its variants. A nasty woman, a female dog, a complaint, or, the verb form—to complain: (*Rapidly.*) Bitch, bitch, bitch, bitch, bitch or even more confusing—try this one: an adjective—BITCHIN', Man, those boots, they are BITCHIN'!

In the right mouth, it's a compliment.

But not in his mouth. That guy—the guy this morning, driving a Volvo, for God's sake, what's the semiotic significance of that? Huh? The sign and the signified? Or the signifier and the signal, or—I mean—A guy in a Volvo, balding, pink in the face, glasses, fist in the air, yelling, "BITCH."

There's something to that.

And so even though he's hurling a word we all agree is meaningless, really. Somehow when it's floating in the air, at you—a floodgate opens in the back of your brain, and all those nasty chemicals that you've been reserving for your appointment with the IRS auditors are suddenly seeping into every synapse and the blood in your neck shoots up like mercury in a heat wave and you realize: I'VE JUST BEEN INSULTED! And you're not going to take that. Not from a guy in a Volvo.

Bitch—root word of Ambition. I just wanted to take a left turn. Simple. Okay, I'm turning against traffic, but it's legal. Right? I have an aim, a desire—a wish—a goal. An ambition. Turn left. And the guy coming toward me. He has a simple need as well. Turn right. Left, right, left. BANG! I mean he saw me, I signaled, in fact, I was right there, ready to turn before he had reached the intersection and what does he do? He hits the gas.

35

Like turning fast is the answer to this problem. Get there before she does. JUST WHO IS AMBITIOUS HERE?

Maybe if I had some testosterone in my system, I'd have done the same thing—speed up, get yours before he gets his, right? Isn't that the way things are done in this MAN'S WORLD! Huh? Whoever dies with the most toys wins. Right? That's the way to power, that's the way to the top of the slag heap we call corporate America. Right, left, right, get the hell out of my way I'm wearing a pin-striped suit! I carry a briefcase stuffed with reports I don't understand. I can bullshit my way through a board meeting—I can plow my way through an intersection without causing a collision because—I'M A GUY.

So of course, I hit the brakes. What, you think I'm stupid? He wants to TAKE the right of way fine, but he's not taking my front end with him. BUT what happens is: He can't quite. Make it. So there we are, both in the middle of the intersection and whose fault is it? Mine. Because of my ambition. To turn left. And up goes the fist. And up comes his finger—and that word flies out of his mouth.

And off he went. And there I was. Right behind him. Following him. After that exchange, it occurred to me: I had an opportunity here. Because it is a given that in the hallowed halls of the corporation, she who walks behind THE MAN has no power, but on the freeway, she who drives BEHIND the JERK can scare the hell out of him.

So I just pressed down on the gas pedal . . . and zip! I'm on his tail at 80 miles an hour laughing like a maniac. You think THAT was bitchy, pal? I'll show you BITCHY!

I pull up, close enough to see the white of his terrified eyes in his rearview mirror. My knuckles gripping the steering wheel. My teeth bared and clenched—like a samurai without the sword—veins popping—and it occurs to me: (*Beat.*) What must I look like? And then I see—up ahead, he has picked up a car phone and is talking to someone. And unless he's president of Smith Barney and he's about to lose $400 million on a megadeal—

it's no business call. He hangs up. He's glancing backwards, his eye are wide and there's sweat trickling down his fat pink cheek.

Now, what's the most frightening thing in the world to a man like that? An ambitious woman! Who knows how far she'll go to get what she wants.

Think about it. *Think* about it. Even now. After all these years. Gloria Steinem is eligible for Social Security, half the freshman class of every law school in America is female—and I—I can qualify for a home loan all by myself—yet, we women are still interlopers in the land of ambition. Why else would "bitch" be such a horrible word? If "ambitious" were not a label to be avoided? Let us admit—in a place like this, we're just strangers in a strange land, still learning the rules, still climbing that ladder, still bumping our heads against that glass ceiling without the smarts to cut a hole in it. And what do we do? Climb down.

Bitch is the thing you never want to be. No matter how ambitious you are.

So I ease up on the gas, thinking about it. Thinking about my pink glossy lipstick and the 10 o'clock meeting and absolutely terrible example I am setting for my six nieces and nephews if they could just see me. And the arrow on the speedometer ticks down. Seventy-five. Seventy. Sixty-five.

And then I hear it. The sound that makes your blood run cold. The siren.

I didn't see him. I swear. Think I'm that stupid? Tailgating some idiot at 80 miles an hour with a cop behind me?

Okay, I'm thinking. Just pull over. Tell him what happened. This guy—you wouldn't believe what he did. No—that's no good. Don't confess to road rage. All right. CRY! Cry if you have to! I've done it before—I admit it—I have cried to a traffic cop and he tore up the ticket! It's true. I've traded on my sexuality to get something most guys couldn't get in a heartbeat. Unless the cop is gay. Which he wouldn't admit to anyway. But come on—there's got to be some compensation in life! So I take a deep breath. Close my eyes, think of England. Get ready. I hear the footsteps on the gravel. A light tread. I open my eyes. And there is the stern countenance of Officer Michaelson. Officer Judy Michaelson. Shit.

And Judy Michaelson is not a happy camper. Not this morning. She's looking at me with an expression that can only mean: "You total idiot. I am going to shred you now."

Well you know the drill—the forced politeness of the state trooper to the moron behind the wheel. That sinking feeling of despair. Nothing you say or do will sway this one. And we know why, don't we?

Officer Judy Michaelson is tough as nails. Officer Judy Michaelson cuts slack to no one. Officer Judy Michaelson doesn't dare. Not if she cares about her career. Not if she's ambitious.

She writes the ticket. Her expression hasn't changed the whole time. That look of contempt. Officer Judy Michaelson doesn't care for pink lip gloss. Officer Judy Michaelson knows what the lip gloss is for. She has seen the magic that lip gloss has worked on her colleagues—the men. The ones who can tear up traffic tickets without fear of being called "soft." She hands me the ticket. And then, for the first time, a little smile works its way across her plastic face and she says, "Take it easy."

Bitch.

The Connie Saxon Show

Ethan Kanfer

Scene: A suburban home circa 1960, or thereabouts

Serio- comic
Connie Saxon (30s–40s), a suburban housewife teetering on the verge of a nervous breakdown.

Connie's world is slowly unraveling. One of her comforts is writing in a journal to her dead aunt. Here, she describes a day spent in a garden that is no longer hers.

CONNIE: September twenty-fifth. Dear Daphne, . . . Clark made the vacation speech again tonight. I think when he makes those promises, he really means it at the time. But it never seems to materialize. Anyway, we both know going away isn't going to solve things. We'll have to come home sooner or later . . . I do sometimes think about going away, though. Being by the ocean. Being by myself. I could never get away with it, of course. But that's what I daydream about. Going somewhere far away, all alone. If I told that to Clark he'd get upset. He'd think it strange that I would want to get away from my family, as if it meant that I don't really love them . . . I wonder sometimes if he ever reads this journal when I'm not looking. Probably not. He isn't curious enough. Part of me wishes he would read it. That he'd care enough to invade my privacy. . . I wonder what he'd think if he found out I was writing letters to a dead woman. Maybe he'd yell, but I doubt it. Most likely he'd take the book away and burn it or something, and tell me to pretend it never happened and I should never mention this to anyone. (*Pause.*) He's certainly been drinking a lot more since he took that promotion. I've tried to tell him what I want is a husband who's crazy about me, who wants to touch me all the time, the way it was when we were newly-weds. Instead of a man who's always buying me things . . . I can understand how he feels, though. I know I used to complain a lot when we were living in the city. And he's right, of course. We're a hundred times better off today. But everything was so much simpler back then. It seemed that way anyway . . . Sometimes Clark thinks I want something, when all I'm trying to do is have a conversation. Like the time I told him I'd been working in the garden all day. How I'd been down on my hands and knees, pulling the weeds. How I had done such a thorough job pruning the rose bushes. What I didn't tell him was how good it made me feel. How I was suddenly full of oxygen and light. How I felt I had a talent that the world could use. But somehow I just couldn't find the words to say those things to Clark. Whatever I say comes out sounding either like a complaint or some crazy rambling. So I changed the subject, asked him about his day. How are things at the office? The next day we had more or less the same discussion. After that I didn't bring it up anymore. Well, that weekend it was our anniversary. I thought Clark would forget, but instead he surprised me by announcing that he had hired a gardener for me . . . I couldn't bear to see his face if I told him that was the last thing I wanted. So I acted pleased. I jumped up and down. I threw my arms around his neck and kissed him. He was convinced. And now Victor comes twice a week to tend the garden. He's a nice man and he does beautiful work, but it's not my garden anymore. (*Pause.*) Yesterday, even though it was gloomy, I thought I would sit in the garden while I ate my lunch. When it began to rain I got all my things collected and I was about to go inside, but then I decided I wasn't ready to leave the garden. I walked around feeling my hair coming undone and my clothes getting damp. I looked at all the plants one by one, remembering their Latin names. *Rosa Sempervivens, Covallaria Majalis.* I noticed how the roses were a completely different color without sunlight on them. I closed my eyes and brushed the backs of my hands and the tips of my fingers over the rose petals. And then I opened my eyes and stared into the centers of the flowers watching the droplets collect and form into puddles and overflow out the sides. And then I spread my arms like a bird and started spinning around and around, and slipping, and falling, and getting my clothes dirty and not caring, and feeling the sting in my eyes and tasting the bitterness on my lips because my hairspray had dissolved and it was running down my face. And I took off my shoes and I was feeling the slippery grass and how warm the earth was underneath and I was running and jumping and running and running until I was soaked to the bone. (*Short pause.*) And then I stopped abruptly and realized I had to go inside. Not because I was cold, but because Janet Haines and Bindy Riley can see my garden from their houses, and they are both big gossips. (*Pause.*) That night Hedgehog brought in the plates and cups and soggy sandwich bits that I'd forgotten. He didn't ask me any questions. Funny how he takes after me not his father . . . Next time I go to the garden, I will pick a nice white rose for you. Love, Connie.

Darla

Christopher Woods

Scene: a bedroom

Serio-comic

Darla (50s), a woman coping with loss.

> *Darla's husband, Billy, walked out of her life eighteen years ago. Since then she's managed to find some comfort in an unusual bedtime ritual that she here performs.*

DARLA: (*Looking at photographs.*) Every morning, I dust them both. I turn Billy's picture face up again while the coffee's brewing. I look at Billy and I look at Elvis. I see the sun coming up outside the window. I start another day.

(*Directly to audience.*) I never give up, not me. Yes, I know it's been eighteen years since Billy walked out the door. He didn't say boo. I don't know where he went. He's never called, never even sent a postcard. Mama, when she was still alive, always explained it to me this way:

(*In her mother's voice mimicking.*) "Darla, he's gone to sow wild oats, honey. You let him down somehow."

(*In her own voice again, to audience.*) Between you and me, Billy didn't have any wild oats. Billy wasn't too good with the tame oats either. (*Chuckles.*) But we got along. What I'm saying is this. Billy was no Casanova, not by a long shot. I always figured he'd come back when he figured this out. Or when enough women told it to him, maybe not so sweetly. I loved him because he was Billy. For me, that was enough. Still is. That's why I won't be surprised when he comes back. He'll find out, no one loves him like I do.

But it's strange. Elvis has been gone a long time too, but it's not the same. Oh, I've known the sadness, don't misunderstand me. Who hasn't? Call me crazy, but I think Elvis was a giant among men when he was alive. Now that he's gone, he's still about ten times bigger than most of them. (*Beat.*) You think about it. At the café, I work the lunch counter. I see men coming and going all day long. Some nice. Some give me the creeps. Some try to flirt. But I'm older and wiser now. I know better than to get involved again.

(*She removes her slippers, placing them on the floor.*)

There was a time I didn't know who Elvis was. Mama changed all that. I must have been thirteen, and she took me to see him in concert. She said we had come along too late to see Jesus. But we were right on schedule for Elvis. Going to that concert changed me, I don't know else how to say it.

(*Removes her robe, drapes it across the end of the bed. Yawns.*) Excuse me, but it's late. Some nights I stay up, thinking that Billy is coming home. Call me a fool. If he did come home, it would be dusk. That's how I've pictured it. Coming up the road, the sun a fiery red in the trees. Lost people need to come home before dark. At night, they can't find their way.

(*She reaches to turn Billy's photograph face down.*) Good night. Billy. I'll try again tomorrow. (*To audience.*) Look at him, never changing. And me? Oh, you don't want to know. You can see for yourself. (*Beat.*) Later, if you should tell someone about me, please be kind. (*Reaches for Elvis photograph, holds it close to her.*) It's one of those lonesome nights, honey. The dark seems to slip inside and put its arms around you.

(*To photograph.*) Make it go back outside, okay? You know how to do it. For so many years.

(*As lights slowly dim, she kisses the photograph, then slowly, reverently, places it on the table, face up like before. She straightens the pillow and lies down.*)

Eat the Breast

Lindsay Price

Scene: Here and now

Serio-comic

Naomi (60s), a woman whose daughter is facing a second battle with breast cancer.

When asked why she gives her daughter, Ruth, an appliance every time she gets bad news, Naomi makes the following reply.

NAOMI: I was in a department store, just after . . .

[SIMON: Horses. I got it.]

NAOMI: And I was walking by the audio/visual section—and there was this wall of televisions: forty TVs all with the same program on. Forty voices. Forty faces turning at the same time. I always find that so startling. So many people staring right at me. It was just before the holidays. I was walking by and I was startled by the wall of Jimmy Stewarts. Forty Jimmy Stewarts. *It's a Wonderful Life.* My husband and I watched that movie every year. Sometimes we liked to cheer for Mr. Potter, Lionel Barrymore's character, but that was in the privacy of our own home, no one saw it but us. So I was startled by forty Jimmy Stewarts speaking and moving and I couldn't turn away. The salesmen kept asking me if I wanted help, if I needed anything, very nice young men with red faces and new blazers and . . . I just stood there. Must have been over an hour. A crazy lady in front of a wall of TVs. I saw the salesmen out of the corner of my eye conferring by the stereos about who was going to be the one to escort me out. A young man approached me, the one who drew the shortest straw I guess, all red in the face and before he said one word I slapped my hand down on the nearest thing. I bought a VCR.

[SIMON: Just so he wouldn't throw you out.]

NAOMI: What if someone saw me? Naomi Boyle escorted out of a department store? I couldn't live that down. I was going to take it back. But a week turned into two and three and one night I was so tired of staring at the box sitting on the middle of the floor and I just was so . . . at . . . and I ripped it opened, spilled everything out onto the floor. It stayed like that for a long while. Every night I would sit and look at this thing. VCR. I lined up all the parts, the cable, and finally I looked at the directions. I don't think it was written by someone who spoke English. I spent hours at a time going through the directions. Trying to figure it out. That darn machine made me so mad. I wanted to throw the whole thing down stairs so many times. But every night I sat on the floor and before I could blink, it was time for bed. It was almost . . . soothing in a way. There wasn't any room in my head to think about other things. It took me four months to get it to work. But I did. I figured out how to hook up a VCR and I can tape my shows when I'm not there and I can re-set the time when the power goes out.

The next day I bought a coffeemaker that you can program at night and when you wake up the coffee is made. I had an answering machine which was fine, but now I have one that is inside the phone, it is so easy to check your messages. I have one remote control for the VCR, the TV, and the stereo system. I can work them all.

[SIMON: I don't recall Ruth ever telling me that her mother was so technologically inclined.]

NAOMI: I'm getting up the nerve to buy a computer with a CD ROM and unlimited access to the Internet. I didn't know exactly what to get Ruth. I wanted to . . . She doesn't have a TV.

[SIMON: It would take her longer than four months to work a VCR.]

NAOMI: Ruth and I . . . we don't . . . we never . . . I do know some things. I know that she thinks. She gets trapped by her thoughts. Ben never thought about anything, he was a doer all his life. Ruth and I, we think. There isn't anything wrong with that. Thinking is good. An active mind is what keeps you going. My grandmother lived to a 100 because she played bridge every day. Sometimes, you get trapped. You need a VCR to balance things out.

Eat the Breast

Lindsay Price

Scene: Here and now

Dramatic
Ruth (40s), a woman battling breast cancer.

Ruth cannot face another crippling round of chemotherapy and has determined to run away. Here, she returns from the airport and explains why she couldn't bring herself to get on the plane.

RUTH: I couldn't go.

[SIMON: Why not?]

RUTH: I had my ticket. (*She laughs.*) It's the stupidest thing. I had my ticket. I went through security. I waited for my flight and I couldn't go. They called my name three times.

[SIMON: It's OK. You're safe now.]

RUTH: No you don't understand. I couldn't go but I couldn't come home either. I sat in my chair and watched the airport move around me. I mostly watched the people. People with children. Big Families. I never had children. I didn't avoid them necessarily, I just never got around to having them. Of course no one said to me twenty years ago, "Hey cut your chances and pop a couple." Nobody said: children, no cancer. No children, cancer. I watched people smoking, inhaling chemicals, eating red smarties; I'm sitting there watching people do all these things and I can't even stand up to go to the bathroom. I am paralyzed. So I change my mind again. My mind is made up. I have to come back, make another appointment, go through whatever. I have to come back, go to work, go to Spain. Let the doctors do what they want. Easy. But I can't. I can't. Do you remember my Aunt Ester?

[SIMON: You used to take her Christmas shopping.]

RUTH: I did. My sister did. My mother did. The Boyle curse. Once a year I'd have to go to the home, bundle her up, and go through hell. All those shopping trips where I was supposed to have the upper hand, cause I'm the one with all my marbles, and she'd end up biting a sales clerk, or banging someone on the head over a box of chocolates. She didn't do the respectable thing of disappearing when she died—NO—she's in my dreams. She's on my shoulder at the airport telling me how I'm screwing up again. "Ruth, can't take the pressure? Ruth, by the time you make up your mind it's going to be too late." She's taking away all my power. I can't think. I can't do anything. She's moved inside me, eating her way from stem to stern. Competing with the cancer to see which of them can kill me first. I am being consumed inside and out and I can't stand it!!!

Echoes from the Street

Corey Tyler

Scene: Here and now

Dramatic

Mother (30–50), a woman whose son has been murdered.

Here, a woman who has just lost her child to random street violence expresses her grief.

WOMAN: I hear him . . . in the mornings. I hear his voice coming from the bedroom. Calling me. Calling my name. And he's saying *"Mama. . . Mama you make breakfast yet Mama?"* And on the mornings I hear him I whisper *"Yes. . . yes Son . . ."* I have to stop myself from walking to the room and lying on his bed. Because I know . . . I know that if I step through that doorway . . . if I walk to the room and see his face inside that frame . . . I'll spend my whole day crying for him. Because he's in there. *I know he's in there.* I can feel him waiting for me. Waiting for the breakfast I made him. Waiting for me to answer.

It's a part of you that dies with them. That part you give them when they're born, that life. And that's what you see in the pictures. That's what you feel in the clothes. That's what you hear calling you in the mornings. That part of you that's dead.

I remember the morning he was born . . . lying there with the incredible pain running down my back . . . holding his father's hand and hearing him say to me over and over again *"It's okay . . . it's okay—you can take this . . . just a little longer . . ."* And I did. Because I knew that after all that pain, I knew I would have a baby in my arms. And that I'd hold him and love him for the rest of his life.

And I can still see his face. I can still hear him crying. I can see his footsteps, his first step . . . coming toward me. And I can see him lying there. Not laughing. Not moving. Not alive. But if I walk to the room . . . I can hear him. I can hear his voice. I can hear him calling me. And he's saying, *"Mama . . . why ain't I alive. Why ain't I living Mama? Why?"*

Echoes from the Street

Corey Tyler

Scene: Here and now

Dramatic

Girlfriend (15–19), a young woman whose boyfriend has just been murdered.

> *Here, a relatively tough-minded urban teen struggles to find an appropriate outlet for her grief.*

WOMAN: You know what I hate? I hate the way they try and make you talk to some councelor whenever this shit happens! Don't nobody I know want all these nosy bitches in our business, so who's all this shit supposed to be for anyway? *"Talk to me, talk to me"*—Fuck you with all that talk to me shit! They don't know shit about what's going on here . . . and they're only around for a week anyway, so what do they care? All they want you to do is cry in their face so they can feel like they're doing something! Like this stupid old lady they sent me today . . . asking me all these dumb ass questions 'cause I went with him like *"How are you dealing with him being gone"* or whatever. Like she cares about me an' shit. She just wants to see me cry. . .!

It was a Tuesday I think, the first time. Yeah . . . it must have been 'cause I remember he was walking into mister whatshisface's class late. That stupid English teacher that be kicking people out for shit, like if you sleep in his class or something. *"Class wasn't so dull he wouldn't be having to kick people out!"* He was late 'cause he was talking to one of his boys in the hall and forgot what time it was. But he was probably just out there acting stupid . . . 'cause all the boys I go to school with, all they do is act stupid.

Melanie liked him too. Only fight we had was 'cause of him. See she had tried to talk to him but he didn't want her, he wanted me! And the only time she ever talked shit to me was this one time . . .

Me and him was in the hall after Spanish and she saw us talking and got up in my face an' getting all loud an' shit in front of everybody, calling me a bitch or whatever, saying I took her man and all this bullshit! And I was like *"Look, we could just talk about this shit, there's no need to be screaming at me in the hallway after class, let's be civilized about this at least, y'know?"* But she didn't want nothing to do with me after that. We're cool an' shit now . . . but we didn't talk to one another for a long time after. Too long.

The thing about him though was that he wasn't like all them other punks I go to school with . . . thinking their hard an' shit. And he wasn't like they made him in the paper. He was smart. I mean he was raising his hand up in math class and always answering questions and stuff. And when we had to do a book report and everybody else's was like two pages, his were always like ten and twenty pages long. It was weird being with him 'cause I never thought someone like that would want to be with me . . . somebody smart. But he liked me . . . and I really liked him.

I found out about what happened to him from one of my little brothers. He came in my room right when I was falling asleep that night saying he'd heard somebody had been shot up the street from where he lived while they was on a bike. I asked him what street they lived on, 'cause they probably been in trouble with someone before. But I know he didn't get into trouble with nobody. They just shot him for nothing.

It's hard for me to cry when it happens now. The first couple time's that's all I did . . . cry. But after so many people I knew started getting killed, I couldn't. After a while though, when I got home, after I was thinking about him for a while, I started crying. I didn't cry in front of that councelor though. I'd rather talk to one of those crazy old men that be jabbering to themselves at the bus station than tell her anything. Besides, if they really cared about how kids were feeling, they'd be here for us all the time . . . instead of just a week.

Eulogy: What I Would Have Said, Given The Gift Of Articulation

Daphne R. Hull

Serio-comic

Nonie (85), a wild woman from Appalachia reviewing her life in a nursing home.

> *Here, the irrepressible Nonie ruminates on stairs, Sandy the Daschund, and her second husband, Gig.*

NONIE: You know that death is closing in when you move the bed to the first floor. If folks who put together those statistics were truthful about the main reasons people go to nursing homes, it wouldn't be because of strokes, or Alzheimer's, or dementia, or broken hips—the Number One reason people end up in nursing homes is—(*Game show host.*) Survey says—? Stairs! Stairs, the last bastion of independence! No matter how bad off you are otherwise, you can stay home, as long as you can climb them stairs. I loved our little house. Don't get me wrong, I did—but in retrospect, I would have bought a different house, because it just had too damn many stairs. I would think, given how people are growing older nowadays before they die, that people would stop building houses with stairs. But, people keep buying them, I guess—and that is what it is all about.

Gig—that was my second husband—he tried to keep me at home, moved the bed downstairs—even when I was sleeping in the hospital bed, he slept right in our bed right in the same room—him and Sandy—Sandy was our dog; well really Gig's dog—Sandy was a dachshund who replaced Sweetie—who was a dachshund—after Sweetie passed away. Our family did that a lot, replaced beloved things with new things similar to the old—I guess we don't like change very much. Now, we know they're different, the new things, we're not fooling ourselves there—and they're never quite as good as the old things—but they help, they really do. Every time I needed a new kitchen table I tried to find another one just like the one I had, even if I bought it used at a yard sale or at the auction. Gig wore the same pants, either green or navy or brown, for years. Always wore button-down shirts with them. Never saw him in anything else, except his birthday suit. Hee hee hee!

Eulogy: What I Would Have Said, Given The Gift Of Articulation

Daphne R. Hull

Serio-comic

Nonie (85), a wild woman from Appalachia reviewing her life in a nursing home.

> *Nonie feels death starting to close in and wonders about the things she never tried in her life—like pizza.*

NONIE: You know, I never in my life ate a pizza. I think they're the most beautiful damned things—but I never had one. Never had cause to eat one. I wonder what they do taste like?

When death is closing in, people think about the strangest damned things. What regrets do I have? What would I do again if I had the chance? What didn't I get around to doing? I never ate a pizza. I never traveled abroad. Julia says if you can't find happiness in your own backyard, it ain't anywhere to be found. I guess that's true. I never worked in an office. I never had children of my own. I never graduated from high school. I never saw the ocean. I never knew anyone famous or rich. I SURELY wasn't ever rich myself! Never had no need for it!

What did I do? I was married—twice. To good men. I worked hard when I had to, not at ALL when I didn't. I bought a house. I lived in a small town where everyone knew me and I knew everyone. Not more than 400 people in that town! I survived TB. Survived a sanitarium. Drank, and danced, and got rowdy when I was young! Ooooh, I tell you, I was READY. Kept the house and the dogs while Gig worked on the railroad. Went to yard sales and auctions and bought every little thing I liked. The little house out back is full of stuff I bought—and the big house, too—little pink dogs that bark and walk, lava lamps, clocks, a table lamp made out of popsicle sticks, glassware, hamster cages, golf clubs, bibles, tools, candle holders, cigar boxes, smoke eaters, necklaces, pictures of Jesus, a bust of John F. Kennedy. He's in the living room—J.F.K. Right on top of the color TV. Some might say it's junk, but it's MY junk, by God!

Now J.F.K., he was our last good president, in my mind.

The funny thing is, I don't think I would try a pizza if you put one right down here in front of me. Huh!

The biggest scandal ever happened in Sharpsburg, as I remember it, was when Kathy Bender—another Kathy, and Bender, not Benner—now, this isn't my fault, this is someone else's family, not ours—when Kathy Bender run off and married that black man. He was fairly nice, for a black man, but she was a WHITE GIRL. And while you see that more and more nowadays, you just didn't see that back then—and you STILL don't see that there in Sharpsburg. Poor soul, she brung him back home with her—well, no one would talk to her in the whole town. She finally left. I think it nearly broke her heart. People are just—mean. Not to me. But people who are mean to me, I don't pay no mind anyway. You can't, to survive in this world. You just can't.

You know death is closing in when you're full of advice for other people on how they should live. Experience! Huh!

Being cooped up in this one room has got me thinking about all kinds of things. Like this window here. Window to the world where I ought to be. All I can see through it—when they actually open up the drapes for me—is a parking lot, some trees, some sky. It's not much, but it's more than I've got now, in here. Looking out windows is kind of like looking at your family: You figure, there will always be time to get to that later. There's another day to go to the auction with Dootie, another day to have the kids over, another day to clean the porch, another day to go to the place you see in that window—until one day, everything is different—you have a catheter shoved all up your private parts and your mouth doesn't move right when you try to talk and suddenly your husband and your seventy-two-year-old baby sister and eighteen-year-old girls treat you like some sort of—of CHILD or something! One day you have all your choices, the next day you don't have any. The next day you get a stupid stuffed dog that smells like piss instead of a real dog. The next day you end up in a room that smells like Lysol with no husband and no couch and no one you recognize. The next day your excitement is built around red Jell-O with bananas, a SPECIAL treat. The next day you think to yourself, huh! I sure as hell don't remember looking through THIS particular window. How the hell did I end up here?

Eve Of Crimes: Memory Motel

Bob Jude Ferrante

Scene: A church confessional

Dramatic
Tabitha (34), intense and soulful; a woman who has suffered and has been irrevocably changed as a result.

> *Tabitha has been ritualistically raped and beaten by Axel. Here, she recreates the horrific experience in a church confessional.*

TABITHA: OK . . . 1992 . . . PR firm . . . So! We're about to pitch Combustion Engineering. They make cooling systems for nuclear power plants and they are, yeah, three million bucks worried a year. Mavica—my boss—goes, "Tabitha, girl saving Allied's five point five million dollar ass means Mavica, Chicago, Mavica, Chicago and leaves Mavica no time to write her killer Combustion proposal . . . Tabitha, you gotta pull me from this fucking pisshole sewer and write it, the one, the slam dunk. Please." We're talking *late*. Eleven PM. Ever hear of this shit?

[PRIEST: Well, people *die* at eleven PM. Sometimes later.]

TABITHA: (*Gets all up in the confessional door, visibly excited by the mention of death.*) Who's dying? What's that supposed to mean?

[PRIEST: Uh, last rites.]

TABITHA: Oh, But it doesn't get you *promoted*, does it? (*Beat.*) So it's done . . . I'm heading through the dark parking lot to my car . . . thinking how utterly killer my proposal is . . . I mean, what kind of idiot walks alone in a dark parking lot, with her mind on something else?

(*Axel enters from offstage and stands in the shadows. We can make out greasy coveralls and a wrench. Throughout this scene, Tabitha speaks for both Axel and herself, alternating voices as indicated.*)

(*In Axel's voice.*) "Tabitha! My savior!"

(*In Tabitha's voice.*) Oh man, Axel. My ass is dying for a hot tub.

(*In Axel's voice.*) "Only take a minute. The damn van, engine's like a stone. Can you ever? I said to you about Alecia. She is a good van. You just gotta hold the wheel while I roll 'er over. Otherwise, Alecia, she just roll on toppa *me*."

(*Pause.*)

(*In Axel's voice.*) "Please."

(*Tabitha fumbles in her purse.*)

(*In Tabitha's voice.*) Here. Take my Triple-A.

(*In Axel's Voice.*) "Come on. It's eleven. You know how long Triple-A takes? You're layin' in your bed smilin', I'm freezin' my tailpipe two hours in this parking lot."

(*In Tabitha's voice.*) OK . . .

(*Pause.*)

(*In Tabitha's voice.*) If I ever need a Six PM pickup . . . I'm talking a last minute pickup here . . . I receive *no* shit from *you*?

(*In Axel's voice.*) "Ow."

(*In Tabitha's voice.*) Going once.

(*Brief pause.*)

(*In Axel's voice.*) "She's parked over here."

(*She walks as if going to Axel's van.*)

(*In Axel's voice.*) "Thanks so much, Tab. Like I said, you my savior."

(*In Tabitha's voice.*) My name's Tabi-THA.

(*Awkward silence.*)

(*In Axel's voice.*) "Sit there and turn the key when I say."

(*In Tabitha's voice.*) Let's go.

(*In Axel's voice.*) "You can't rush it. With cars, it's timing, timing, timing."

(In Tabitha's voice.) What is that smell . . . gas? It's like—whew!

(Tabitha turns around, trying to see behind her. She mimes that a man's hands have clamped a rag around her nose and mouth. Axel twitches as she moves. Then, darkness and silence for a moment.)

I woke up—

(Lights.)

—my arms to my feet . . . hog-tied . . . in back of the van. Crickets. Axel over me, dark across his face like . . .

(Pause.)

I said something *brilliant*, like, "Hey what the fuck?" He said,

(In Axel's voice; now Axel echoes what she says, word for word, quietly in the background.) "At this point she is not possessed of the expertise necessary to speak, so perhaps she might want to listen. What does she say?"

(Tabitha mimes trying to get up.)

(In Tabitha's voice.) What did you do to my legs, motherfucker?

(Struggles. Neither her arms nor legs move.)

(In Tabitha's voice.) They're broken.

(In Tabitha's voice.) Help! Help!

(Tabitha recoils as if slapped.)

(In Tabitha's voice, Axel softly echoes her.) "He tries to explain to her that flesh is the same. But she does not listen."

(In Tabitha's voice.) Somebody else is here?

(In Axel's voice, Axel echoing.) "See? She wants to ask questions. No expertise."

(Tabitha mimes being smacked hard in the face.)

They say "I saw stars." They got it right. I figured things out pretty quickly then.

(In Axel's voice, Axel echoing.) "A muscle relaxant. This is a substance that causes no permanent damage. She should relax and finish her date."

(In Tabitha's voice.) Date! Not likely, asshole.

(In the background, Axel raises his arm.)

(In Axel's voice, Axel echoing.) "She could make a leap here. An intuitive leap. But will she? No, she will not." He put the gun to her . . . my . . . head.

(In Axel's voice, Axel echoing.) "In the movie he does not hold her where someone could hear a scream. In this case. He chooses a dark woods. At night, the owls turn their heads. Do you like Robert Browning? I love Robert Browning."

(In Axel's voice, Axel echoing.) "Oh, sir, she smiled no doubt whene'er I passed her; but who passed without much the same smile? This grew. I gave commands. Then all smiles stopped together."

(Darkness. A single, horribly loud slap in the dark. Silence. Lights. The confessional. The shadowy figure of Axel is gone.)

The guy who picked me said he saw this woman—me— blood all down her torn skirt, jerking along the roadside. He took me to the hospital. Days go by and the cops show. The detective says they're guessing assault, would I confirm. No, lieutenant, I kicked my own ass. They ask, press charges? Press?! *Pound* the charges—! *(She mimes pounding a stake into a vampire's heart.)*

—Into! His! Fucking! Heart!

(Tabitha takes a breath.)

So: mug shots, sketches, bad coffee. Cops track employee records. And guess what? They *catch* the sick fuck. He's working in an office. Already has his eye on a new girl.

(Lights fade as she speaks so her last words are shrouded in darkness.)

But now someone has their eye on him.

Eye of the Beholder

Heidi Decker

Scene: Here and now

Serio-comic

Fiona (30–40), wealthy, elegant and southern.

> *Fiona has always relied on her beauty to open life's doors as she here relates.*

FIONA: (*Looks at audience a moment, smiles.*) I'm pretty. There's no getting around it. I just am. Pretty.

Pretty is more than just a state of being, it's a way of life. My Mama always said, you're either pretty or you're not, and there's no in between. She doesn't believe in bisexuals either.

(*Pause.*) She doesn't like indecisiveness in *anyone.*

So I . . . am pretty. It's what I am. It's who I am.

Now if you're waitin' for me to get to the part where I wish things had been different, that I hate the superficial world that we live in and beauty is only skin deep, you can forget it. Those are just things that ugly girls tell each other to make themselves feel better. (*Tilting her head at audience.*) Now you know it and I know it. There's no need to pretend for me.

This face, and this ass, have gotten me everything I've ever wanted. No, I didn't get things with sex. I am far too well bred to be that vulgar. Besides, I don't have to. "Pretty" is the promise of sex. Of good things, better things. I am the trophy that's just out of reach . . . that gleaming, glistening thing that's always *juuuu-ust* beyond their fingertips . . . and people will do anything to get a glimpse, a taste, a touch. I'm the fucking Holy Grail! (*Laughs.*)

(*Smiles kindly at audience.*) Don't talk to me about being objectified. (*Aside.*) Yes, I *am* able to use four-syllable words. Bein' a woman never kept me from getting a thing.

Now it's not that I don't empathize. I *do*. I've read plenty about the feminist movement . . . and I feel sorry for them, I do. But I don't see what any of it has to do with me.

I mean, c'mon, let's be honest here . . . *(Lowers voice a bit, leans forward.)* . . . we all know that those people are just women who were never quite pretty enough. Now that's not *my* fault. The truth is the truth, and if it hurts I can't help it.

(Matter-of-factly.) I didn't make the world. Mama always told me, God made the world and it is how it is. People like me are born this way. These looks are God given . . . and if God decided to make me better than some people, it is not my fault.

She warned me all the time when I was a child, and she was right. The world has always been filled with people who are jealous of people who were born better. Like . . . like royalty and peasants! Look all through history! It's all the same. It's decided when you're born, and that's it.

I have worked very hard to maintain *this*. People have no idea what it's like to be me. And those people who get all that surgery to try to look like people like me . . . well *that* is just the saddest thing. It's like people who buy themselves a royal title. Oh, it seems impressive at first, until you get in a room with someone who's the real thing.

My Mama was *very* brave. She took a huge risk when she had me. *(Pause, sincere.)* Well, what if it had turned out that I wasn't like her? Can you imagine? My mama is what is known as a classic beauty. She and my Daddy were so brave . . . who knows how I could have turned out. I mean, the doctors can only do so many tests . . . beyond that, you have to just have faith that God will keep you.

Mama says she cried and worried and prayed for months. She even had a couple of prayer vigils with the women in her bridge club . . . and . . . here I am. Mama's reward!

I inherited just about everything from her. Well, except one thing. *(Pause.)* I'm not so brave.

The Imp of the Perverse

Tami Canaday

Scene: Here and now

Serio-comic

Rhonda (30s), a woman confronting a Peeping Tom.

When Rhonda catches up with the man who has been peep-ing at her house, their conversation leads her to confess that she too indulges in a bit of voyeurism while on the job.

RHONDA: Everyone's ironed. I just got this big worker iron and the cord hooks to a pole running across the ceiling.

[JOHN: Go on.]

RHONDA: This iron moves along a pole, like this. *(She demon-strates.)* It's as light as moving your hand across a man whose got no chest hairs. The ironing board is by the register, so I run the register too. Customers bring in their dry cleaning and I count it for them. One pant. Two dresses. A tie. A muff. You know, one of those things you put your hands in? *(John nods.)*

RHONDA: Customers don't notice me. There's this man who isn't married. He don't have a wedding ring and he's got these eyes. The best eyes I've ever seen. He's come to the shop for years. I know his shirts and his pants. I iron them extra spe-cial. I put creases in them, the starch is generous, but he don't care. He never says nothing about it to me. He rushes in, with his car keys a jingling, and wants his dry cleaning now. His name is Teranova. Don't know his first name 'cause we only ask customers for last names and numbers . . . phone numbers. I got his number and I called it once. I was gonna see if he wanted to get a drink or something, but I hung up before he answered. He don't know who I am. He comes in every Monday after lunch and I talk friendly to him and he looks right through me. "Hurry up, I got me important things to do." But he always comes back. Mostly, the customers don't notice me.

(John stands and tucks in his shirt.)

[JOHN: I notice you.]

RHONDA: My ironing board faces Colfax and I've done ironing so long, I can watch the street and iron at the same time. I like Colfax Avenue 'cause it's a shifting all day. It can be crowded and then nothing. I've even seen weeds blow down the street for a long stretch . . . like in a cowboy western. The bus stop is near my window. Either folk are hot or freezing. I see them in the winter stamping their feet and blowing on their hands. Come summer, they're quiet like, not moving. It's too hot. There's no middle ground at a bus stop. I should know. I take it enough. Colfax is like TV for me.

Jane: Abortion and the Underground

Paula Kamen

Scene: USA, the 1960s

Dramatic
Crystal

> *In the 1960s, a woman's rights group was established in Chicago and was known only as "the Service." It's purpose was to provide safe illegal abortions to women in need. Here, Crystal recalls her experience with the Service.*

CRYSTAL: I was a sophomore in high school and I attended Rezin-Orr High School on the West Side. It was located on Augusta and Keeler. It's on Pulaski and Chicago Avenue now. One of my high school chums came to me and told me that she was pregnant, and she said she had to get an abortion. It wasn't like thinking that maybe she should put it up for adoption or what have you. She said that she had to get an abortion. And I was a virgin, you know, so I was just supportive. So I said, OK, I would support her. What happened was she did all the contacting. I don't know how she found the organization, but she came to school one day and said, "I found someone to give me an abortion—and I have an appointment set up."

So, I think that we even took public transportation to this house . . . And we went to this apartment and there was a couple, a white couple and (*With some confusion.*) . . . I believe it was the South Side . . .

Well, they started to describe what the procedure would be like, but I'm sure the first thing they did was find out how pregnant she was, what her age was, trying to determine, you know, if she was a good candidate . . . And so I think we asked how much or something and they said there's no set fee, but whatever you have. She had fifteen dollars. I remember that. And so she gave them the money, or however the arrangement, I don't know. (*Nods head.*) . . . But I know she had fifteen dollars.

But we started crying at some point while she was talking to us because we were so young. We asked if I would be able to go with her, and that's when they told us that they had a place that I could go to while the procedure was taking place.

Well, I remember her, you know, saying that in terms of when it happened, that it was painful. You know, that she cried and that whole thing because she went through that alone . . . I don't know if she ever told (her parents), but I know it was very traumatic, and it stayed with me. I don't know how this woman could ever forget.

Jane: Abortion and the Underground

Paula Kamen

Scene: USA, the 1960s

Dramatic
Sunny (18–20), a feminist activist and artist. Her memories of the past are clouded by drug use.

Here, a vibrant young woman recalls the harrowing experience of going through with an illegal abortion.

SUNNY: *(Concentrating on remembering.)* I started coming here (to Chicago) when I was fifteen, and I was finally able to stay when I was seventeen. I had myself declared an emancipated juvenile in family court. Something not a lot a people know about, but what kids can do to get away from abusive families . . .

Oh, yeah. I know where I was living then. I was living above this costume shop on Cleveland and Lincoln. It's not there anymore . . . My landlord owned the costume shop. I'd work now and then as a waitress, the usual stuff.

(Pauses.) I did not want to marry the baby's father; I didn't even want to see the baby's father anymore. I didn't want to have a baby at all. When I was growing up, pregnancy outside of marriage was almost a death sentence. It was terrifying . . . And our choices were unwed mothers' homes. You know . . . When I was fourteen, one of my older sisters had a baby and had to give it up. Because that's how it was then, 1964, in a small town. And she never, ever recovered from that. She's almost fifty years old (now) and she never got over it. The shit we went through.

. . . And I explored some people. A couple people gave me some numbers of illegal abortionists. I called them, and they were like, "Yeah, my name is Bernie. I'm the one who does it." And it was terrifying. It was absolutely terrifying—the thought of dealing with these people.

And then I saw this ad. It said, "Pregnant? Need help? Call Jane." It was something like that, in an alternative newspaper and it just looked interesting and I didn't know why. I didn't know anything about it, and so I called.

She invited me over to her house to meet with her. And I went to her house and I was immediately comfortable with her. She had a daughter that was about four or five and the house was really homey. There was like laundry folded on the couch. It was an apartment in the Old Town area. She turned out to be the sister of my next-door neighbor—which really helped me a lot. It made it easier for me to trust her. She was a hippie housewife. Really nice person. The kind that really makes you fell at ease. She didn't treat me like I was a case. She treated me like I was a person. She didn't give me the social-worker type treatment, you know?

She wanted to know real basic stuff, how far along I was, if I had seen a doctor, if I had considered having the baby . . . if I was sure about that's what I wanted. And I think she took a medical history for me there. Asked me about drug allergies, the usual stuff they ask you about before surgery. . .

I only met with her once. I don't know if I should have had more or not, but I was so far along and they wanted to get me right in there. . .was about four and a half months pregnant. That's what I had been told. But when I actually had the abortion, the doctor said that I was further along. So, I was in the fifth month.

(Switching topics.) I was in a real weird situation and I was really isolated . . . Yeah, I lived alone. I spent a lot of time alone. That's what you do when you're an artist. You work in a studio by yourself . . . I was a painter.

(A doctor and nurse begin to set up an abortion operation on the other side of the stage.)

I was freaking out. I was trying to find a way to take care of it. And I was also trying to get money together. I didn't have any.

69

. . . Yeah, I mean, it was kind of scary. Because she told me it was going to hurt. She was real clear about that, that I might be scared and that things could go wrong, but they would take care of it. She said if there were any complications, they would take me to an emergency room, that they would take care of me. And not just abandon me, so. . .

They told me to go to a certain address at a certain time and I went there. It was in an unfamiliar neighborhood. I remember I met there with a bunch of other women and new counselors I hadn't met before. . .

(*Pausing.*) At an apartment, I think. And they took us in a van to another building. We couldn't see out of the van and we were brought in the back way so we couldn't see the address or where we were. And that's the apartment where the abortions where done . . . I think there were two doctors—that's what they told us they were—in two different bedrooms. When it was my turn— we were watching the women come out of the bedrooms and they were pretty woozy so we were real scared. I heard people crying sometimes. I tried not to listen.

So, (a woman) came and took me into the room and explained to me again that I would have to be blindfolded to protect the identity of the doctor.

(*Patient six is led into the room, and she lies down on the bed.*)

. . . And, so she blindfolded me and she sat next to me and held my hand and talked to me through the whole thing. The doctor came in, he examined me, he got pissed off because I was further along then I was supposed to be . . . And then he started dilating me and did the abortion, which was incredibly painful because I didn't have any anesthetic at all . . . Nothing. . .

(*Doctor C. enters and begins the procedure.*)

And, the doctor was a jerk . . . He was making remarks about me crying and what a big baby I was—and he was an asshole and I kind of told him off at one point.

[PATIENT SIX: Are you done yet? Are you done?]

SUNNY: I wanted to kick him. I didn't do it.

[DOCTOR: Not yet.]

SUNNY: I told him he was an asshole. I said, "How do you know how this feels?"

[DOCTOR: I just have to make sure it's clean in here so that you don't have any problems.]

SUNNY: You're a man. How do you know what is supposed to hurt and what isn't? He said, "I'm a doctor."

[DOCTOR: This is for your benefit.]

SUNNY: I know this stuff.

[PATIENT SIX: I just . . .I gotta get outta here.]

SUNNY: I felt sick. You feel sick afterwards . . .

[DOCTOR: Just a few more minutes.]

SUNNY: I must have been feeling bad because I started doing a lot of drugs after this . . .

[DOCTOR: Just relax.]

SUNNY: . . . and that's why it's hard for me to remember how it happened. Having a child then would have just destroyed me. There was no way that I could handle that. Emotionally. In any way. I was totally unequipped to have a child. I could barely take care of myself. If it wasn't for Jane, I don't know what would have happened . . .

Killers

Werner Trieschmann

Scene: Here and now

Serio-comic

Mary Ann (30–40), a woman struggling to balance the violence in our society with the violence depicted in film/TV and the violence in her own heart and mind.

Here, Mary Ann relates a tale about a recent video rental.

MARY ANN: You know I saw that movie, one of those very disturbing movies that put me off all TV and film for a while. It's rotten what's comes on the screen and I believe that even though I used to be very wild myself and sort of a late hippie though I did bathe and didn't quite believe in free love because that's what men wanted. So, you know. One night after the end of a very long week of houses that did not sell and family problems that you would not believe if you saw them on a talk show, I decided to rent a movie. Escape in the form of video cassette. So I stumbled into the store and picked something off the shelf and stumbled out again. I don't even ask those pockmarked clerks behind the desk because I don't want to be in the video store on a Friday night all by myself one minute more than absolutely necessary. And why they have the brightest lights in those stores, I have no idea. It's like walking into the middle of a circus ring and you're the Chinese baboon with the bright orange ass. So, you know. As it happened, I've rented this movie where this woman is burned alive. While I can identify, I don't want to see it in full color and blaring at me on the screen. We get the picture of her trapped in the coffin and banging on the coffin lid, which was all because she was nice to this man at a truck stop, which was her first mistake and you should never make eye contact at those places and everybody is well aware of that. That's a fact of modern life. Trucks stops will get you *killed*.

Listening to Insomnia

Amy Beth Arkawy

Scene: Here and now

Serio-comic

Sylvie (50s), a women contemplating violence in society.

When her husband is mugged, Sylvie spends a sleepless night wondering about the future.

SYLVIE: He sleeps. *(Sigh.)* Just look at him. Like a baby. He drools like a baby. But he snores like I don't know what . . . an emergency overtime Con-Ed construction crew at five o'clock on a Sunday morning. The point is he's sleeping. Like nothing happened. Okay, the first two, three nights he paced a little, drank a little warm milk with a shot of whiskey so it shouldn't be a total loss. But after that, in bed lights out right after Sue Simmons closes up shop on the eleven o'clock news. Like always. Not me. Me—I'm up every night for thirty-two nights half fuming at him for being able to sleep, and half worrying I'll have no one in that bed to fume at tomorrow.

The thing is: Nothing happened to me. It was him . . . Mr. Big Shot carrying cash like it's the good old days who goes and gets himself mugged. He says, "It's nothing Syl. It happens to everybody." Nothing? I don't call being held at gunpoint by two schvartzes and a spic nothing! I know, I know, I shouldn't use such language. But, really, the neighborhood's gone to hell in a handbasket. And no one can tell me different.

I told him—I've been telling him for years—"Bernie, let's get out of here, move to Westchester. Get a nice house, with a lawn, maybe a pool, live the good life." The business is doing well enough. God knows, liquor always does well. And the way he does it—all cash—Uncle Sam doesn't have to know all the details, if you get my drift.

But he says the store's here. "If you don't watch the register they'll rob you blind." Not to mention his mother—pushing ninety and mean enough to outlive us all just for the fun of it—won't budge out of her rent-controlled rattrap.

(Beat, pacing.)

Not that the suburbs guarantees anything nowadays. My sister Bea knows this woman—lives in a big Victorian on the tony side of Larchmont. Well, some guy busts in at four AM, pulls three or four computers out of the wall, smashes them to smithereens, goes into the master bedroom, turns on the TV, full blast so a Court TV special on some serial murderer is blaring all the way down the block, and then, get this . . . he throws a machete at the headboard. Misses them by this *(Gesture.)* much. A machete? Where the hell do you buy a machete in the suburbs? Where the hell do you find a machete anywhere? It turns out, the guy lived down the street. He was a bipolar day trader. NASDAQ took a dive, he threw his Lithium out the window and went bonkers!

So what can you do? We're all on borrowed time from here on in. Midnight January 1, 2000—I was drinking champagne . . . Dom Perignon . . . just in case, why leave the good stuff behind? Anyway, Bernie gets it wholesale . . . and playing Hearts with Bernie and Maude and Phil from next door. I shot the moon, sixteen, seventeen times easy waiting for the planet to blow up already.

So what's with God giving us an extension? For what? I ask? What's left? We should just elect Jerry Springer president and be done with it. Or Charleton Heston . . . he'd get the job done faster, if you get my drift.

(Beat.)

So tomorrow, he'll go back out there. And I'll sit inside waiting and worrying and watching people kill each other all over the TV. Or maybe I'll surprise everyone and go out myself. Do something different, maybe even a little daring. I could get a tattoo.

Or get my sagging nipples pierced. Or buy a gun.

Mercy Falls

Jeni Mahoney

Scene: A hospital room in Mercy Falls, Ohio. Christmas Eve

Serio-comic

Wanda Moore (30–50), generally adored author of inspirational books.

> *When Wanda is visited in the hospital by a fan, she admits to having fictionalized her "true" stories. In fact, she steals her plots from the lives of others. Here, the crafty writer tells the tale of her first inspiration.*

WANDA: All the people in my books are real, they just aren't really me. Listen, Marcy, I was born with a gift. A talent to write and to inspire people, but I had nothing to say. Can you imagine the tragedy of my situation? My life was absolutely uneventful until that fateful day when I met Little Molly Mabel and realized my true destiny . . .

[GERMAN LADY (*Unseen*.): Mit der Reife vollendet sich die Frucht!]

[MARCY: Little Molly Mabel?]

WANDA: The circus freak turned secretary . . . with the third hand growing out from the bottom of her foot . . .

[MARCY: The inspiration for Hand Under Foot!]

WANDA: She was so brave. After spending years on the sideshow stage, to let the doctor remove the third hand was risking her very livelihood. Who knew if she would make it as a secretary, when I met her she didn't even know how to type! "Molly," I said, "you should write a book about yourself!" But she just couldn't see the heartbreaking beauty of it all, not the way I did. Besides which she had no talent. *None* whatsoever. And that's when it hit me, I, Wanda Moore, could make a masterpiece of Molly Mabel's story. So I did!

Hand Under Foot sold out as fast as they could print it, and from all over the world—letters! Letters from people who were inspired by *my* story, and I knew from that moment on that this was what I was meant to do. Of course I'll still always wish that I was more like you, Marcy, with my own personal tragedies to overcome . . .

Moonshades

Wayne Paul Mattingly

Scene: A home in N.Y.C. suburbia

Serio-Comic

Ann-Marie (40s), a woman struggling to reinvent her life.

Ann-Marie's husband, Hallie, has been having an affair for the last twenty or so years. In an effort to remain in denial, Ann-Marie has tried everything from dance lessons to writing a book. When Hallie finally 'fesses up and asks for a divorce, Ann-Marie is stunned.

ANN-MARIE: Your father came by this morning . . . Is there coffee? My mascara's a mess . . . He took me to breakfast at the Tin Roof. I don't want to look like a pig in front of him so I ate that frozen tuna sandwich before he came.

[MOON: There. Right there. Mr. Coffee.]

[GINA: Did you thaw it?]

ANN-MARIE: He told me . . . he wasn't staying. He told me he wanted a divorce. He sat there eating his greasy ol' bacon n' sunnyside eggs—with all those customers there—an' he says it's not workin'. After twenty-three years. I know you all think I'm stupid an' crazy—

[GINA: No one ever . . .]

ANN-MARIE: All those months away, year after year—I may be crazy—I've always been crazy for Hallie—But I'm not stupid. *(Shift.)* He ate everything on his plate—cleanin' it with his toast n' dunkin' it in his coffee—he *never* finishes. And there I was, crying, watching him smoke his ugly cigarette—as far away as a picture screen. Finally, I said, "How long have you been seeing this woman?" I'm not stupid. "Twenty years," he says, "give or take," smoke comin' out of his nose like Humphrey Bogart, like he stepped off the movie screen. Usin'

77

his sexy voice, like the smoke . . . She's been around almost from the beginning . . . And no one of you, ever told me anything. I wanted to be . . . Part of this family but, no more . . . no more. Blood. *(Shift.)* Comin' through this door . . .*(Pause.)* Not a word. Even my own children. No wonder you treat me like a fool. I think I'm going to throw up again.

The Most Fabulous Story Ever Told

Paul Rudnick

Scene: Christmas Eve

Serio-comic
Rabbi Sharon (30s), an aggressively confidant, gung-ho lesbian; a cable TV diva, wheelchair bound.

> *When Sharon encounters Steve, a bitter HIV-positive man who denies that he is God's victim, she lays the following rap on him.*

SHARON: Come off it. You think about God more than anything else in this room. Why you? Why now?

[STEVE: No, I don't!]

SHARON: *(Physically pursuing Steve, in her wheelchair, really going after him, picking a fight.)* And why not? God made you sick! And not your neighbor, not some fascist dictator, not some creep.

[STEVE: It's a virus!]

SHARON: Come clean, baby! It's God!

[STEVE: Fuck you! And fuck God!]

SHARON: Now we're talkin'! Siddown! *(Steve hesitates; he doesn't sit. Gesturing to her wheelchair.)* I am. *(Steve, grudgingly, sits. Sharon moves her wheelchair into a position to face the group.)* Five years ago, it's Sunday morning, and I'm walking down Christopher Street, on my legs. And I've just done a bat mitzvah, for my gorgeous niece, and I'm carrying my latte, my heavenly date-nut scone, and the Sunday *Times*, and I'm headed back to see my naked young girlfriend. And then—a bicycle messenger. Outta nowhere, he swipes me, my legs go out, the *Times* goes flying, and I'm slammed smack—into the back of a Fedex truck. Which doesn't see me, so I'm lying in the street a broken hip and five fractured ribs, it backs up onto my pelvis. Fedex truck tires! And then—it goes forward, right in my ribcage—crack! And by this point, people are screaming and pointing and then, and I swear, I am not making this up, I am a person of God—a rusty air conditioner falls off a twenty-story building, onto my face! And, as I finally lose consciousness, thank you, I see that bicycle messenger *eating my scone*!

And I come to, three weeks later, paralyzed, half-blind, and I think, what the fuck is going on? Not just why me, but why the fucking air conditioner? And some nurse gives me this book, called *Why Do Bad Things Happen to Good People*. And all I'm thinking is, I don't care! What I want to know is, why do *good* things happen to *bad* people! I'm in a wheelchair, and Saddam Hussein's in a Mercedes. I can't walk, and O.J.'s on the ninth hole. I'm paralyzed and Brooke Shields has a series!

And then—it hits me. What doesn't? Why it happened. And what I'm supposed to do, with my useless legs and my messed-up life and my deluxe new nose—do you like it? *(She gestures to her nose.)* "The Mindy." So I buy me some airtime and I say, listen up, New York! Take a look! *(She gestures to herself and her wheelchair.)* This is your nightmare! This is the ice on the sidewalk, the maniac in the hallway, this is God when she's drunk! So if I can believe, if I can still thank someone or something for each new day, if I can pee into a bag and still praise heaven for the pleasure, then so the fuck can all of you, mazel tov, praise Allah and amen!

My Vicious Angel

Christine Evans

Scene: The psychological inner space of a woman who is paralyzed

Dramatic

Pearl (20–30), a fallen trapeze artist, who is confined in a spinal brace.

Here's Pearl's mind wanders through dark mazes of memory as events from her past compete for recognition.

PEARL: *(Whispering.)* Dad? *(Pause.)* I know you're there. You hate being stuck too, don't you ? Landlocked . . . I'm more like you Dad. We need air rushing past us . . . (*Singsong.)* and a star to steer her by. The highlights . . . *(Pause, then sardonically, struggling again with bar.)* Melbourne Age: The highlight of this otherwise tame and tawdry circus was Pearl Watts's sizzling flying trapeze act, which flaunted the aerialist's erotic thrall with death. That's crap, it's with *life*. Kick start the heart so it beats and beats like wings, lift me up, lift me up—I was pretty hot Dad, hot enough to single the walls.

(Wind effects stop. Pearl hits a wall of pain that restrains her.)

Aaah—I hate walls. Walled in by skin— *(Muttering.)* Going stir-crazy . . . We're like sharks, eh Dad. Have to keep cruising. Keep moving. Eddie was always on me, "Why don't we settle down somewhere Pearl?" Settle down—yeah, like lead in the pockets of a corpse.

(Pearl is tired from the bar, but still restless.)

Once they start up with that stuff, I'm off. "Better to burn than to last," hey Dad? *(Distorted crackly salsa drifts in, as if from a faraway radio on a breezy day.)*

(Sings a bit.) Salsa the night away, sleep until midday. *(Speaking.)* But I never did find the bird market. Must have moved since you were there—a *(More like child, quoting Dad's postcards.)* The fabulous African phoenix. The marmoset dance.

The monkey with his sticky paws . . . I have Buenos Aires too, Dad. *(Pause.)* 'Cept when the rain belted down on the roof for weeks, and it leaked . . . Everything went moldy. Endless bong sessions and cards . . . *(As if playing 'Snap.')* Snap!

(Salsa music stops abruptly.)

So much smoke in the room, like having a pillow over your face—snap, have to get some air.

(Bari sax begins menacing pulse.)

Outside, get a grip, roll a cigarette—but when I take a drag, the tip of my roll burns a hole right through the sky. Sky starts peeling away like really thin skin. And then Ed comes out after me, can't breathe 'cause the sky keeps burning and peeling, layer after layer and he goes and puts his arm around me, then I really can't breathe— "Isn't it beautiful" he says, and I go "Wha-wha-wha" like a car that's trying to start and he goes "The dawn—but the sky looks like it's got leprosy," then I start thinking, all skin's like that, just dead flaking layers, I can feel his arm around me, dead skin cells rubbing off on dead skin—yuk—

(Bari pulse stops.)

Anyway, it didn't work out with Eddie.

(Dad [accordion effects] is silent.)

(Anxious.) Dad? Sorry, I went on a bit.

(Pause, then accordion plays wind and water FX.)

That wind in the rigging. I could heat it up on the trapeze. Even miles from the sea. Sailors have to be away a lot. Like me. Not a 9-to-5 thing, our line of work. A rope breaks, you fix it. A big storm, drop anchor. Have to stay flexible. Not bloody land-locked like this.

Never the Same Rhyme Twice

Rooster Mitchell

Scene: A remote cabin somewhere south of Buffalo, New York, on a chilly October evening

Dramatic
Sam (40s), a tough woman confronting her life's nemesis.

> *A friendly game of poker between girlfriends turns ugly when Tommi, who is married, declares that single Sam is out of her league based upon Sam's lack of experience with men. Here, Sam makes the following reply.*

SAM: You guys remember my mother?
[CHARLIE: Your mother?]
[JO: Sure.]
[TOMMI: What about her?]
SAM: *(Moves about.)* I remember when I was a little girl, she lost her job at the auto plant. Her boss told her he was tired of lookin' at her, that she was too old, washed up at forty-five years old. My mother was rugged, beautiful; she worked her fingers to the bones . . . and in return, got nothing but put-downs and sarcasm and a pink-slip *one* day shy'a Thanksgiving. I remember she used to call a rejection a *rhyme*, said it sounded more poetic, more palatable; all based on the notion that there's poetry in power; *great* poetry in power, of which she had none. Those in control, she used to say: Those are the ones dishin' out the rhymes. *(Continues to move about.)* Well. One rejection. One rhyme. That's all she knew because she was cunning and careful the rest of her life. She got another job and worked there for thirty years. She retired gracefully, gold watch and all. She always taught me to be

aware of situations where I could get hurt; be it work . . . romance . . . whatever . . . that it's the suckers of the world who hear the same rhyme twice. *(Beat.)* I'M alone because I got left at the altar five years ago. That was *my* rhyme. *(Moves to Tommi.)* So don't you *dare* tell me I'm out of your league, sister; 'cause when you get right down to it . . . you're out of *mine*.

Officer Justice

Janet Pound

Scene: Here and now

Dramatic

Police woman (20–30s), African American, exuding deadly philosophy.

Here, a pragmatic young police officer describes her own kind of personal justice.

OFFICER JUSTICE: You don't know. You don't see what I see. Live what I live. We come from different worlds, you and I. I'm the one that makes it easier for you to sleep at night. You don't even want to know what I see in my dreams.

I should shed a tear for some son of a bitch who would rather cut my insides out than say hello to me? It ain't gonna happen. *(Pats gun on belt.)* This baby is registered to the Detroit Police Department. And this one; *(Pats back pocket.)* isn't! Unregistered. Keeps it clean. It's a piece like this that killed the strung out drug dealer that had a knife to my partner's throat. Second-generation trash. Not immoral. Amoral. Whole lot worse. They'd kill you for a dime and laugh with their daddy about it. And I should feel remorse? Never.

Do you really want us to treat the scum of the earth to our candy-coated court system? Do you want your tax dollars going to some bullshit juvey home so this disciple of Satan can sleep well before he gets out and has another chance to blow away your loved ones? No, siree.—

Have you ever held a crack baby all jerkin in your arms? Seen an old couple tied up with fishin' wire, fear so embedded on their faces that the mortician can't wipe it away? Tried talkin' with a catatonic twelve-year-old victim of a gang rape? Police brutality? I'd say angels of mercy; putting those mad dogs out of their misery.

Next time you're readin' your morning *Free Press* over coffee and wonderin' about another body found in the river. Don't give it no mind. No thought at all.

Party Story Prisoner

Janet Pound

Scene: Here and now

Dramatic

Eishe (20s), an Iraqi-American who longs for the freedom promised to her by the American Constitution.

Here, a young immigrant reveals her unhappiness with the new life her family has found in the United States of America.

EISHE: I came here years ago with my mother. Too young to remember Baghdad. Yet my mother tells me story after story, more than I care to hear. She needs me to listen. But I want to scream, please stop. I've heard it so many, many times.

My father worked ninety hours a week in his brother-in-law's party store on Detroit's Northwest side, to save the money to send for us. Cash in boxes under the bed. In Iraq no one trusted banks. Ten years without seeing his wife and child. How do you make up for that?

We came like all those before us, for religious freedom, and a better life. We left a country where Muslims persecuted us for being Chaldeans—Catholic Arabs. And came to a country that persecutes us because they think we're Muslims.

My mother won't complain, she respects my father but I know how lonely she is. She aches for her friends, her homeland. She doesn't speak English. When they call us Camel Jockeys and desert niggers and laugh, she doesn't understand. I say "Oh moma, they're just being friendly," and she smiles at them. She only wears black. It's customary for women to wear black for a year after a loved one dies. Eventually it becomes an older woman's uniform.

"Eishe," my father says, "smile, be happy, we are together, free." I cannot tell him I don't feel free. I feel like a caged animal pacing back and forth behind the glass and bars among the bottles of alcohol. Land of the free? This bulletproof glass was my sixteenth birthday present. I want to tear it down but I promised my mother I wouldn't. Three of our relatives have been shot, killed, in their stores.

I want to study art—paint colorful landscapes, beautiful scenes—but my father believes school is only to prepare a person to make a living, and I already have a job, in the store.

I have two aunts waiting for us to send them the money to come. It is my turn to sacrifice. I want to write to them and say stay, stay! The winters will chill you to the bone. Your souls will grow cold. You will hear gunshots in the streets just like in the war. We showed our allegiance by sending our boys to fight in Desert Storm, some fought their own cousins. And in our stores when our backs were turned like cowards eggs were thrown. Home of the brave?

We don't ask for handouts. We take care of our own but still there's little tolerance. Maybe when I have children their days won't be spent gazing on cigarette cartons and empties. Maybe they will live in beautiful gardens and paint and dance. For them I will go. But for now, there is no leaving because of the sorrow I'd put in my mother's eyes.

The Power of Love

Sebastian Michael

Dramatic

Jo

JO: come back one second
now you listen to me
why would I care for what you wish
where in your mind is the window that looks out on the
battlefield
that is my life
and prompts you
of all people
to raise your little white flag and say: hey: let's just be friends
how does it matter to what
you
think is best
why do I have to be put here on the spot to listen to what
you
of all people
have to say.

now you have got one thing upside down my girl
one thing you do not understand
you're right: i'm angry. i'm angry and hurt and cut up and i
hate
what's happening to me
but there is one thing you do not understand:

i love tender.
i have loved him every day since i met him
i've loved him when I shouted at him
and i've loved him when i felt his hair against my breast

i've loved him when he farted and i've loved him when he
brought me flowers
for my birthday
i've loved him when he snorted a grand we were meant to spend
on holiday
and i've loved him when he gave me my child
and i still do
i still love him
i still love tender
but I can't
i can't
see him any more

because i can't look him in the eyes
it's too hard
it's too hard for me
to look him in the eyes and miss him
to look him in the eyes and
miss him at the same time

it's
too

hard

can you understand that

The Power of Love

Sebastian Michael

Dramatic
Jo

JO: no no tender
i'm not into rhetoric
i don't ask
rhetorical questions
i need you to realize something for me
i need you to realize that
wanting me there for you in sickness of the heart
craving my familiar body for comfort
looking for me to make it go away
that
alone
is not love
it's need
you are in need tender
you give me
need

but what *i* need
is love
i need a love that i can
build on
and depend upon
because, because people who need me
i have three wards full
at the hospital

that
is why i'm leaving you

it's not because you've screwed around
i could probably forgive you that
once
it isn't even because you've given me the virus
though i haven't forgiven you that
and it isn't
it really isn't
because of the child.

other women have lost their child
and made it through to the other end
it's not because I've lost my child tender
it's because i've lost you.
[TENDER: I don't want to go.]
JO: but you already have gone tender.
you already have
you'll have to come back to me from a lot further away
than eugen's place
and I don't know if
and when
that can happen
[TENDER: I don't want to go.]
JO: tender
listen to me
shhh
listen to me
i haven't got the strength now to be angry with you
i haven't got the strength now to shout and scream at you and
kick you out
i want to
but I can't.

so i'm asking you
please
tender
take the bag

leave the key
and exit

please

please
tender

please

The Power of Love

Sebastian Michael

Dramatic
Jo

JO: you see
you're on target

that's a very different place to where i am

i
have been in mourning, eugen
of course I went to work every day
of course I kept going
i do
i'm built that way

but i've been mourning
for
I don't know
probably for my future
because I had one you see
i had a good future

tender and i had a good future lined up together
i
i didn't just get pregnant you know
that wasn't an accident
I'd made a decision
with tender
we'd
decided
to give it a go

we always decided to give it a go
right back when he took me out to the dogs
our first date
he took me to the dogs

we ate chips and shared a can of irn-bru
and put money on hounds with the craziest names
we didn't win anything
but we had a good laugh all the same
and we decided to just
give it a go

we did well from deciding to give it a go
each time
each time right until last summer

i was looking forward to having a child with tender
i knew of course it would be a bit like having two boys to look
after
but I never needed him to change for me
i didn't
i just needed him to be a good part of my life

and he was
he very nearly was

you know he phones me almost every week, sometimes twice
even now
after ten months

i never answer the phone
i just listen to his messages
why do you think that is
because i don't want to speak to him?
because i don't care about him any more?
because i've given up on him?

that would be easy
it would be easy to find the words for that
if I could actually hate him for what he's done
if I could hate him

god that would be easy
i'd find the words for that

what i can't find the words for
is saying to him
i believed in you
and you let me down

because it means i was wrong
it means i was sure of you
and i was wrong
and i can't bring it back
the being sure

and i *was* wrong
i actually was
i'm not imagining it

i was wrong about tender
and that

hurts

The Quarterly

Valerie von Rosenvinge

Scene: Here and now

Dramatic

Sesily (30–40), a psychiatrist reliving a dark time in her childhood.

> *Sesily has been meeting with her friends to read a play based
> upon an old journal that has managed to dredge up unhappy
> memories from her past that she here shares with the group.*

SESILY: Up in our attic, there was this room. It was apart from the
rest and . . . well . . . one time we . . .

[BROOKE: We being?]

(Kathleen shoots a look at Brooke.)

[BROOKE:*(Continues.)* What? I want to make sure I get the story
right.

SESILY: My uncle and I.

[BROOKE: Oh.]

SESILY: We went up looking for some stuff my mother wanted
and we wound up in the extra room. There was an old brass
bed in the corner and I started jumping on it while he looked
through the boxes. Then, he got on the bed and was bounc-
ing me all over the place. I kept losing my balance and falling
down. I was lying on the bed, laughing, and one time I went
to get up and he told me to stay down . . . so I did.

[BROOKE: Why did you do that?]

[MERIWETHER: Brooke! She asked us not to interrupt.]

[BROOKE: I know, but why did she do that?]

SESILY: I did it because there was no reason not to. I thought it
was cool that somebody his age would want to hang out
with me, you know . . . anyway, I did what he asked . . . and
then he was lying down next to me . . . He started to touch
me . . . I knew it didn't feel right, but he kept telling me

everything would be fine . . .and I believed him. He said he wanted to make me feel good. I looked up to him . . . maybe thought I loved him, I don't know, but I do know that it hurt, it hurt like hell . . . but in some really fucked up way, I guess I wanted to please him . . . so I let him do it. Look, he was my mother's brother and I didn't know it was bad. I trusted him. I was ten years old—give me a fucking break!

[MERIWETHER: Oh, Ses.]

SESILY: After that first time, I didn't say anything. I just wanted it to go away. Then it started to happen a lot. He said he loved me and would never do anything to hurt me. So, you see, I was confused . . . I thought it was me . . . that it hurt because there was something wrong with me. He said people wouldn't understand . . . they would get mad . . . and I would be punished if I said anything . . . so, I kept quiet.

[KATHLEEN: Ses, I can't believe you've never said anything about this.]

SESILY: It was a dark place for me, but you have to know, I got out of it. Every time he would take me to that room, I knew what was going to happen, and I dealt with it . . . or so I thought . . . and then one day when I was fourteen or fifteen . . .

[BROOKE: This went on for five years?]

SESILY: . . . I realized that I could say no. He had threatened me, but I'd seen enough, heard enough, by that time, to realize the truth and I finally had it within me to say no . . . I was not going to do it anymore.

[MERIWETHER: . . . and he stopped?]

SESILY: He never touched me again.

[BROOKE: Oh, Ses . . .]

SESILY: Unfortunately in my mind, it happened over and over and over . . .

Rage Amongst Yourselves

Amy Beth Arkawy

Scene: A group therapy meeting.

Dramatic

Tess (30s–40s), a woman struggling to find a place where she belongs.

> *Here, Tess reveals how knowing that she was adopted alien-ated her from her family and left her feeling empty and root-less.*

TESS: *(Sort of laughing.)* Being adopted is no great shakes, but it's far from juicy. It's about feeling like you . . . I mean feeling like I don't belong anywhere. *(Pause, embarrassed.)* Christ, I sound like I'm on *Sally Jesse Raphael* or something. Let's just forget it. It's not important, anyway. It's ancient history. It's got nothing to do with anything, anyway. It was bad enough not to look like them. But I couldn't even think like them or . . . *(Laughs.)* smell like them. It's crazy, but for the longest time, I actually tried to smell like my mother. I'd sneak into her closet and wrap myself up in her old fisherman's sweater just so her smell would rub off on me. But it never worked. *(Laughs.)* It was this blend of Chanel Number Five, cigarettes, and wintergreen lifesavers. It was sickening, really. *(Pause.)* See, how nuts is that? I wanted to walk through the world engulfed in a nauseating aroma just because it reminded me of my mother. The thing is, I don't think they ever really wanted me, which sounds stupid because when most people adopt a child it's because they really do want one but can't have their own. I think my parents adopted me because it was the right thing to do. Like they were proving to the world, to God, maybe, that they were good people. But they never seemed to want me around. I think they went on a cruise up the Nile three days after they brought me home. *(Pause, laugh.)* It must have been three weeks. Three days wouldn't look good. It's like they traveled all the time. When I was fourteen they sent me to Emma Willard—it's a boarding school . . . And then they stayed home. Now they keep asking me why I don't visit more often. How screwed up is that?

The Rim of the Wheel

Daphne R. Hull

Scene: Baltimore, 1994

Dramatic

Sheree (30s–50s), an African-American woman whose son has been accused of murder.

Here, this exhausted woman is interviewed by a television reporter.

SHEREE: My son and his friend confessed on the TV. You already know what he said. *(Pause; Joanne waits for an answer, gestures her to go ahead.)* They said they asked this man for his money and he wouldn't give it to them. They said they was scared. I'm not saying what they did was right. It wasn't. It was wrong. They sat right there on my sofa and told the world this, right into the TV camera. *(Pause; stares at Joanne; who nods encouragingly.)* But. I know my son Benjamin. He did not do this.
(Elena wearing a black suit, white shirt, and purse, walks on unnoticed, downstage tight. She stops just onstage and listens.)
I don't think he's innocent. I don't THINK it; I KNOW it. He—
[JOANNE: Come now, Miss Williamson, how can you say that? After all, your son DID confess to the murder.]
SHEREE: I KNOW. I know what he said. But MY son—look. My son did not pull any trigger. Yes, he was there, yes he was. But he shot nobody. Not my son. The other boy did it. He didn't shoot that man, the other boy did. He said he did it. All he has to do is say to the judge what he told y'all on TV, and my boy will come home with me. *(Pause.)* I thought about the mother of the victim. I hurt for her. I do. My whole family do. But I hurt for Benjamin, too. I know he didn't kill the guy.

I got him a real lawyer. His life—well. It wasn't the best. I did the best I could, but things are real different now for young people than they was when I was young. Whatever the judge decides his bail is today, we gonna walk out of here and pay it, and get him home where he belongs. I pray for the other boy, too, and for his momma. I pray for the guy who was killed on the street that night. *(Pause.)* I guess I'm jus' prayin' for us all. What else can I do?

The Rim of the Wheel

Daphne R. Hull

Scene: Baltimore, 1994

Dramatic

Elena (50s), a woman whose only son has just been brutally murdered.

> *Elena has risked everything to emigrate from Russia to the United States of America only to lose her only son to senseless street violence. Here, she is interviewed by a television reporter regarding her son's tragic death.*

ELENA: These tears . . . I need these tears. They are part of me now. My son cries out through me through these tears. That mother—it was difficult to watch. *(Joanne listens, but motions frenetically to the cameraman to get the film rolling.)* I don't care, I need to say this for me. And for Igor. Igor—my son—he was my heart. They killed my son, but they killed my heart also. I cannot cry more, but I cannot stop crying. I came to this country to protect the future of my son. They killed not only his future, but a good person, a good citizen. They killed someone who would have a future. I told him he would find his future here in the United States. All my years, I will be guilty. *(Deep breath to keep from sobbing.)* One son, our handsome boy. Why do they take only the best? I'll never, never be a grandmother. Who can understand the deepness of the pain? That mother. I try to—I want to understand her. I saw how she cried. She is crying for her son, as I cry for mine. She raised a killer. I think a lot of people cannot give sympathy to her or her son. She raised a killer. She said his life was not the best. My life—my son's life—they were not always best—what excuse is that? My son is dead. For money. What is the philosophy of this country? My son was killed because he had a job. Because he carried money. Because he wanted to give the money to his boss. After he died, they didn't even take the money. They found it with him. It was less money than it cost to fly him here. So he died for what? Because he had things someone else wanted. There were many things Igor wanted. And he killed no one. I did not raise a killer. *(Pause.)* My son is dead. Her son is alive, and inside that courthouse. He may still go free and have his life. Her son maybe didn't shoot my son Igor. But he was there. He had a part in this. Her son helped kill my son. Her son killed my heart.

The Serpent's Kiss

Jocelyn Beard

Scene: A loft in TriBeCa

Dramatic

Caroline (60s), beautiful WASP socialite, savvy and unflappable.

When Caroline sees that her daughter, Hallie, is on the verge of falling into the same social trap that she has, she reveals her one time crush on Ringo Starr in an effort to encourage Hallie to make a break from tradition.

CAROLINE: Let me tell you a little story, dear. *(Hallie groans.)* No, no. You'll like this one, I promise. Now, although I never did have a romance with your father, I did manage to have one very short-lived romance. It was 1964. Goodness, that was a long time ago, wasn't it? It was 1964, and everything in the world was changing. Even me. Until 1964 I had never even dreamed my life would change until one incredible day when I heard a voice and saw a face and fell in love, for the first and last time in my life. Ringo Starr. When we heard that the Beatles were coming to America, to New York, I thought to myself: This is it. This is my chance to break free of Mother and Father and . . . everything. I'm going to go to Carnegie Hall and Ringo will see me in the front row and he'll know in a single moment that my love is the one thing that can save him from a lifetime of loneliness and despair.

[HALLIE: Oh, Mom.]

CAROLINE: I know, I know. Foolish . . . melodramatic. But it was how I felt, dear. And so I started working on Father until he agreed to take me to the first Carnegie Hall concert.

[HALLIE: You saw the Beatles at Carnegie Hall???]

CAROLINE: I had everything planned perfectly. I spent a fortune at Bonwits on a new dress. It was a pale lime green . . . velvet

105

bodice and satin skirt . . . puffed out like a cloud. It's probably hanging on a rack in some vintage clothing shop in Cold Spring, poor thing. Anyway, I had the perfect dress. Mother wanted me to wear bobby sox but I told her I'd rather die and bought a pair of silk stockings and a lace garter belt and wasn't I just the sophisticated young Manhattan socialite. I wore a pair of black sling pumps and carried a little matching purse. There was no way Ringo could miss an angelic vision like me in the front row.

[HALLIE: But he did.]

CAROLINE: I wasn't in the front row. When we arrived at Carnegie Hall, Father quickly ushered me out of the car and into a side door. I barely had time to see the hordes of girls who lined the street just to get a glimpse of the Beatles. There were so many, and it was so cold. I was introduced to a man whose name I can't remember who was something like the executive director of Carnegie Hall and, of course, a personal friend of Father's. Can you imagine? The wings of Carnegie Hall? I didn't know what to think. I was given a badge, which I had to pin on my lovely dress and told where to stand. It was warm and dark. I felt as though I was wrapped in heavy velvet. All sound was muted and time stood still. There were others in the wings, all standing quietly . . . waiting, just like me, their faces pale and full of yearning, just like mine. And then I heard a noise that chilled me to the bone and drove all that lovely warmth away. The doors of Carnegie Hall had been opened and the audience had begun to rush down the aisles. It was bedlam in an instant. I waited there for what seemed an age, praying that the heavy curtains would keep me safe from that shrieking sea of girls . . . and then, I heard a new sound: It was a wail, a primal banshee wail that rocked through that poor old theater, shaking the very foundation all the way down to the river bed. *They* were there. And I hadn't even seen them come on stage. I'll tell you this, darling, they looked nervous and young . . . very young . . . and they had terrible skin. I took a step forward and I could just see Ringo over George's shoulder . . . behind his drums and that moment was pure ecstasy for me.

[HALLIE: *(After a moment)* And??]

CAROLINE: And then I heard Father say: "Well, at least you're making money on this tomfoolery, Robert." He was shouting, actually. I hadn't realized that he was in the wings, too. They both were, he and the man who gave me this badge. Standing right behind me. I took another step toward the stage, just to get away and then I saw them. The girls. The wailing, screaming, weeping girls. A wall of them. Like a tidal wave, frozen in on its course . . . hovering, threatening to slash over the stage and drown us all.

[HALLIE: Good lord.]

CAROLINE: Carnegie Hall was washed white with the power of flashbulbs and the music that we had all come to listen to was drowned out by the cacophony of the screaming crowd. In that instant I realized several important things, dear. I realized that my Ringo wasn't mine at all but theirs. The Beatles sang their songs for those impassioned screaming young women, not for the overdressed little rich girls waiting quietly in the wings. I realized, too that I had no scream in my own heart. Just a whimper. I knew in that instant that I could never be a part of that wonderfully wailing crowd. It would never have been permitted. Even if I'd managed to get free of my father and his family I wouldn't have had the stomach for it. There is a terrible, ghastly divide in our society, Hallie. You and I stand on one side, and the rest on the other. If you'd married that mythical French industrialist's son you might have had a shot at sneaking over to the other side from time to time.

The Serpent's Kiss

Jocelyn Beard

Scene: A loft in TriBeCa

Dramatic

Hallie (late 20s–early 30s), beautiful WASP, a woman coming alive after a lifetime of numbing privilege.

> Hallie fell in love with the darkly passionate Joe, a killer for the mob who was murdered by Ty, Hallie's vindictive old flame. Ty has blackmailed Hallie into marriage, and although she hates him with everything she's got, she has no choice but to comply. On their wedding day, Hallie goes to the loft where Ty shot Joe and says good-bye to his restless spirit.

HALLIE: (*Softly*) Joe? It's me, Lestat . . . Hallie.
   (Joe enters quietly. He is dead. Hallie cannot see him.)
      I just wanted to tell you, that ever since . . . that day I've decided that I believe in ghosts. You see, I can still feel you, Joe. Your mouth on mine . . . the taste of you. I smell you on my skin and in my hair. So, I believe in ghosts. I believe you're still here . . .

[JOE: Here.]

HALLIE: And I believe you can still see me . . .hear me.

[JOE: In this place.]

HALLIE: I believe these things with all my heart, Joe, because if I didn't, I'd have to kill myself.

[JOE: Then believe.]

HALLIE: I want to tell you some things before I leave, Joe.

[JOE: Tell me.]

HALLIE: First, I want you to know that I am going to kill Ty. I don't know how and I don't know when, but I'm going to kill him for stealing our lives. I don't think you'd hate me for that, would you, Joe?

[JOE: No.]

HALLIE: Then I'm going to buy back this loft and we'll be together.

[JOE: No.]

HALLIE: And, I want to tell you something that I've never told anyone before. I used to hear the jungle . . . all the time. It's intoxicating rhythms all here, in my head. But it's gone now. Since that day. Now I hear only my memory of your voice.

[JOE: Memories fade. You will forget.]

HALLIE: And lastly, Joe, I want you to know that I did burn that day . . . with you. You raised me from the dead and breathed life into me. You swallowed me whole and now my body and soul belong to a ghost. You've become my private god, my Baal.

[JOE: You will forget.]

HALLIE: I have to go. I'll be back, Joe. I promise. I love you, Joe. Always.

[JOE: I want you to forget.]

HALLIE: Good-bye, Joe.

(Hallie takes one last look around and then exits.)

Shoes

Sky Vogel

Scene: A small, upscale shoe store

Serio-comic

Jackie (30s), a schoolteacher with unique insight into life and love.

When confronted with a bitter victim of a failed relationship while shopping for shoes, Jackie attempts to help him get back on track by assuming the role of the woman who left him.

JACKIE: This marriage "thing" . . . Y'know I really have always thought it was a fairly easy concept. Two people get together and agree to create something that they couldn't separately. A family. Not two single people who get a break on their taxes. A family. Not a part-time, whenever-it's-convenient-for-you arrangement. A family. It's what I want. It's what we agreed to.

(Dave looks at her.)

JACKIE: I've had pets. Don't imagine that you are anywhere near as wonderful. Even on your best days.

[DAVE: *(Moving toward her.)* Hey . . .]

JACKIE: And furthermore, explain this concept to me: "I don't know what I want anymore." I'm not buying into that. Who knows what they want anymore when you really get right down to details. But people—adults just don't change overnight. We're not really any different today than yesterday. And when you told me only a *few* yesterdays ago that you wanted to spend the rest of your life with me, to grow old with me . . . Today can only be the same. But I know what it is. You want to be married a little and single a little. You think that's an option. Well guess what? I think you're

wrong. So here's my plan. *I'm* going to be single a lot. And you . . . can play with your little self . . . in hell!
(Pause.)
[DAVE: God, this is . . .]
JACKIE See? Not listening again. As usual. *(Pause.)* Just go.

Small Mercies

Heidi Decker

Scene: A small city park

Dramatic

Henla (20s–50s), a woman searching for something.

> *When she can't find what she's looking for in her bag, Henla makes the following wry observation about perceived loss.*

HENLA: Ow. Damn! *(To audience.)* What?! Oh, like you don't do it. *(Pause, then thoughtfully . . . as if she's finishing a thought she began in her head.)* You know we all feel it. It's everywhere. You're feeling it right now. Every single damn one of you. Every time your mind wanders and you look off into the distance . . . you watch yourself a movie that takes you to another place and you think about it. When you can't sleep at night because it's too hot or you're too tired and you lie there and look at the ceiling for what seems like forever you think about it. And your stomach twists and your chest aches and you lie there and wish you had something else. You don't know what it is but you know that you don't have it. And your throat tightens up and you think, "Daaaamn." Damn. Nobody knows what the hell it is either. That's the kicker. Everybody has a hole in their chest and nobody knows why. They just know it's empty. Most people think they just want what somebody else has got. Tell a poor man that "a man who has friends is never poor," and he'll say "Fuck you, gimme a dollar."

Sweet Butterfly on an Alligator's Lip

Richard Lay

Scene: A mansion in Charleston

Dramatic

Vanya (20s), a waif with animal cunning.

> *Vanya has conned her way into Lavinia's life with every intention of cheating the wealthy widow out of her fortune. When Lavinia puts her on the spot, however, the crafty drifter decides that honesty is the best policy.*

VANYA: I am a liar and a thief and I deserve nothing from you dear lady. I am a worthless fraud, a cheap charlatan . . . brought to you by this man *(Pointing to Pump.)* with the sole intention of trickery . . . I am the lowest of the low . . . feigning muteness with the intention of deceiving you . . . I am not worthy of your spit . . . So, you may ask, why am I speaking out of character . . . Let me tell you. I do so because in the presence of St. Rita, I feel, for the first time in my life, humble—stripped bare of all criminal intent. I throw myself on your mercy. To you, I confess all of my crimes . . . I truly am a hopeless case, a case so hopeless that I was thrown out of my home by my own parents, forced into prostitution by economic stress, violated by unspeakable forces and given to evil thoughts concerning yourself. I had decided to pursue the aim of relieving you of as much money as I could . . . There it is, that is what I have to say, except that I urge you to throw ME into the gutter where I belong. I am not worthy of your roof.

A Third of Your Life

Justin Warner

Scene: A mattress store

Dramatic

Kate (30s), exhausted, consumed with unyielding purpose.

> *Kate is surprised to discover that the mattress salesman seems to know a lot about her personal life, including the fact that her husband left her some five months ago. When the outspoken salesman condemns her husband for having left her, Kate reveals the sad truth.*

KATE: I'm not something you made up. I don't hurt the way you want me to.

[TOM: I know.]

KATE: No you don't. I'll tell you what happened with David. Why I can't sleep. But you're not going to like it.

[TOM: Okay.]

KATE: We went to bed one night. David said he had a headache. I told him to take a couple Tylenol. So he did. I told him I wanted to talk to him about something. He asked if it was his fault. I didn't want to go through that. So I said never mind, just go to sleep, it's okay. The next morning I got up and snuck in the shower ahead of him. I came back and he was still in bed. I went and made scrambled eggs and he was still in bed. I came over to bed and shook him, then I turned him over. There was a trickle of dark blood leaking from his ear. The doctor said it was congenital. A weak blood vessel in the brain. It was just waiting to happen. I came home and the bloodstain was still on the bed. I couldn't sleep in it. I couldn't turn it over. I barely even go in the room. I've been staying up all night, lying on the couch, with the TV and lights on. And all the time the bed has been staring at me, daring me to climb back in, daring me to close my eyes, daring me to stop breathing. Today I was driving back from work, and realized I was in the wrong lane and there was a Buick coming straight at me. And I didn't really care. Fortunately, the guy in the Buick did. When he skidded past me, I felt some kind of flash inside my brain. Suddenly I was awake. So I turned around and came here, and I told myself I wasn't leaving until I got a new bed. So maybe I could sleep. Maybe then I could stop thinking. Maybe then I could stop beating the living hell out of myself. Maybe then I could forget this stupid dead marriage to my stupid dead husband and it would finally be over. But I don't want it to be over, I don't want it to be over. I don't want it to be over.

Threnody

David-Matthew Barnes

Scene: A one-room house in rural California, summer, 1989

Dramatic

Dana (20s), a young woman trapped in a destructive relationship.

*Here, desperate Dana confronts her lover, Jake, with the fact
that she cannot forgive him for raping her at a party.*

DANA: The orchard, Jake. Do you remember that night? I just
remember the dirt. I was laying there in the dirt . . . you were
on me and you kept pushing against me. Your fingers felt like
razors, tearing at me. I could smell the booze on your breath
and it was so sour and it made me gag. I wanted to vomit,
but I was choking on the dirt. The fucking dirt was in my
mouth. And I couldn't breathe. I was fighting you. I was beg-
ging you to stop. But you wanted to come. And I let you have
your way. Then you left me there, in the orchard, in the dark
. . . so I followed you, back inside. Back to the graduation
party where you told all of your friends to be polite to me. But
they kept giving me these looks . . . dirty looks. It was because
they hated me. They were all on Monica's side. I just wanted
to leave! I wanted to claw my way out of that place. I would
have dug a tunnel with my bare hands just to get away from
you and those people. I turned away from them all. I was
standing in the corner and I was staring at the wall and the
music was pounding in my ear. I wanted to reach up and
grab this baby blue streamer and tie it around my neck. And
choke. I just wanted to go outside, even though it was so
cold out there. But I realized . . . that it was much colder
inside. Their eyes and their red plastic cups filled with beer
and strawberry wine and ice cubes. I just stood there. And I
was freezing, and all of their eyes were on me. My dress was

ripped. And I looked down, to try and fix it. And I saw the blood. Jake. It was running down my legs . . . like my soul was crying. Nobody offered to help me, Jake. No one. Not even you. They were trying to get inside of my head—

[JAKE: *(He begins to sob, softly.)* Dana, please don't.]

DANA: They wanted me to hate you because they all knew that you were way too beautiful to ever love me. I was just a speck of dirt on the wall. I was a whore from the city who fell in love with some guy after a slow dance in a cheap bar near the train tracks. They knew what you had done to me. Even though I told you no. Do you realize that, Jake? I kept saying no! But you couldn't hear me, because I was full of dirt!

[JAKE: I'm sorry!]

DANA: You were so messed up that night. I had to drive us home . . . and I was still bleeding. From your scratches and scars. I brought us back here so you could pass out and so that I could wash the dirt out of my hair. And that smell . . . that awful, awful smell of you and their judgment. I can still smell it sometimes. When I'm sitting here and I'm waiting for you to come home. And I'm listening to nothing. Not even to the sound of my own voice. I gave that to you a long time ago. Didn't I, Jake? I gave you everything . . . and you took it!

Vernon Early

Horton Foote

Scene: Harrison, Texas, 1950s

Dramatic
Mildred Early (50), long-suffering wife of a hardworking country doctor.

Years ago, Mildred and Vernon lost their adopted child to his birth mother, leaving them acutely depressed. Vernon has had his work to divert him from the sadness, but Mildred has been forced to face her loss daily. When Vernon rises in the middle of the night to respond to yet another emergency house call, Mildred erupts with rage fostered by sorrow and loneliness.

MILDRED: Hello. Yes. Hello. Yes. Oh. May I ask who's calling? Oh. All right. *(She pokes her husband. He is in a sound, sound sleep and she can't wake him. She speaks again into the phone.)* Miss Ethel, he's so sound asleep it's going to take me awhile to wake him. I'll have him call you as soon as I can get him awake. I know it. Yes'm. As soon as I can. *(She turns on the reading light hanging on the bed, and she turns to her husband, who is now snoring ever so slightly and shakes him with great force. He still doesn't respond and she gets out of bed throwing the bedclothes back angrily, looking at the clock.)* My God. It's three-thirty in the morning. The drunken fools. *(We can get a fairly good look at Mildred now in the darkened room. The phone rings again. She answers it, almost crossly this time.)* Yes, Yes. No. I haven't gotten him awake yet. I know that. Yes'm. I'm trying. Yes ma'm. I promise. *(She hangs the phone up. She lifts her husband by the arm. She shakes him again and again, almost screaming at him as she does so.)* Vernon! Vernon! Wake up! For

Godsakes! *(He still doesn't wake. She lets his arm fall back.)* I am so sick of being awakened in the night this way. There's not a doctor in this town but this jackass I'm married to, will allow himself to be called any time of the night. *(She takes him by the shoulder now and shakes him yelling.)* Vernon! Vernon! *(Vernon begins to stir, he mutters something, she shakes him again and again calling over and over.)* Vernon. Vernon. Vernon. *(At last he raises his head, opens his eyes and looks at her.)*

[VERNON: What?]

MILDRED: My God. You don't hear the phone. You don't hear me. You're killing yourself for these damn people. Killing yourself. And for what? I'd like to know. You've got all the money any man on earth could wish for. And don't talk to me about a doctor's duty. What about your duty to me? I've put up with for nearly thirty years. Getting up in the middle for the night. Waking you up. If it's a doctor's duty, why are you the only doctor in town or the State of Texas, as near as I can make out, killing himself this way? And I wouldn't care if it were for the sick or the dying. But not for those crazy drunk Dennises. You're gonna get killed out there one night getting into the middle of one of their crazy, drunken brawls. *(The phone rings again.)* Oh, my God. There they are again. Vernon, are you awake? You answer the phone. I'll be damned if I'm going to.

Vernon Early

Horton Foote

Scene: Harrison, Texas, 1950s

Serio-comic
Mildred Early (50), long-suffering wife of a hardworking country doctor.

The prospect of a vacation has made Mildred hopeful, but wary as she here reveals to a friend.

MILDRED: I hope we go to Bermuda, but he keeps eyeing some places in Mexico. *(She laughs.)* Not that it makes any difference where we go. He never leaves the ship. The last one we took together was to Bermuda, and when we docked I said I was going ashore to shop and he said he'd prefer waiting as usual on the ship. So off I go and wandered farther than I should and I decided I'd get a taxi, back to the ship, and hailed one and got in and we rode a few more blocks and we stopped and picked up another passenger and than another and by this time I was getting very nervous and anxious and I told the driver I had little time and he told me to relax and not to worry, and he began driving to what seemed like a very strange section of the city and the driver stopped and let one passenger off and then another off and I looked at my watch and the time of departure for the boat was getting closer and closer and then he let another passenger off and then another and by this time I was in a panic, not only did I think I would miss the boat, but I was afraid he was taking me some place to rape me or rob me. And so I began to cry and pleaded with him to get me right to the boat and he turned the car around after giving me the most disgusted look and raced through the town and got me there just in time. My God I was very relieved. And Vernon was scared to death too, although he wouldn't admit it. He was standing on the deck looking at his watch. *(She laughs.)* I just hope, if he decides to go, nothing comes up at the last minute, like a sick patient to keep him from going. When his mother was alive and we'd go to New York or Chicago for medical conventions, she'd call him the minute he got there about some patient that was refusing to see any other doctor and he'd feel guilty and go on back home. "Darling, I'm sorry to bother you," she'd say, "But I thought you'd want to know." The truth is she was jealous of me. She couldn't stand his being off alone with me. Do you know the whole time she was alive he went over to her house every night and sat on the front porch and visited for at least two hours. He expected me at first to go with him. But I soon put him straight about that. No way I said was I going over and sit on that porch every night with his mother I told him. So, I had my mother move here from Brazoria and she built a house just a block away from ours and while he went to sit with his mother I would get in my car and I would pick up my mother up at her house and we'd ride around town until I'd see his car back in our drive and then I'd take my mother home and I'd go home. That went on until his mother died and after she died he began staying late at the clinic, so I was determined not to sit here by myself and wait for him then either and I'd go and get mother and we'd ride around town, until I'd see his car in the drive and I'd take Mama home and come on home. That went on until my Mama died, now I just get in the car and ride by myself.

Wash Out

S. Heide Arbitter

Scene: The laundry room of a New York City apartment building

Dramatic

Philly (20s–30s), high-strung, a woman trying to literally wash away the horror of her brother's suicide.

Here, Philly confesses her need to keep washing her dead brother's clothes to a stranger she's just met in the laundry room.

PHILLY: My brother wants his clothes to smell clean. My brother wants his clothes just right.

[LOGAN: Your brother?]

PHILLY: We bought these clothes together.

[LOGAN: Teddy's your brother?

PHILLY: Teddy says, "Philly do the wash every day, so that I don't have to watch it grow." Teddy says, "Little seeds are too powerful. They have to drown before they swim." Teddy says, "I'm your family, I'm your man, obey what I tell you." Teddy says, "Philly do the wash everyday. Dirt killed mother and father. Dirt will kill you too." So I clean the clothes. I wash day and night and night and day. Teddy tells me, "The spiders have moved next door. Their webs are blinding my eye. Philly, do it better! Philly, do it excellent!" I say, "I'm doing the best I can. You got me chained here nineteen hours a day!" And Teddy makes a cut in his arm, and the blood is on his shirt. I wash the blood. There's blood on my dress. Teddy says, but I tell him, the smell is too strong! I wash our clothes. I wash day and night. It's all over the floor. And he points the gun! His face is gone! And Teddy says, but he's staring at me, and I tell him, but it's all over the walls, the sheets, the clothes and everywhere. Teddy says, "Philly be clean. Let me be proud of my little sister. I want to smile up at my little sister. The only sister I have on the planet. My clean little sister!" In the place where they send me, they teach me to be clean. They teach me to care for myself. They teach me to wash and wash and wash. They teach me to medicate myself and how to stop screaming in the night. They teach me to live. They teach me to do a job I should have done better.

What Corbin Knew

Jeffrey Hatcher

Scene: A VIP hospitality suite in a skybox high up in the entertainment complex of a large second-tier American city

Serio-comic
Thada (30s), neurotic, bohemian chic, funny-shoes-and-granny-glasses type, who is a journalist.

Here, Thada recounts her day covering a tedious suburban book club luncheon.

THADA: Oh, this being without a car is a real hassle. I have had the worst day! I absolutely cannot work in this world. I like jobs where I'm working with people and jobs where I'm working alone, but I don't like doing them simultaneously.

[ARNO: What do you mean?]

THADA: Well, first I had to go to the post office and mail that story— *(To Corbin.)* I'm writing short stories again— *(To Arno.)* —and I was standing in line to get to this surly postal clerk who, when he sees me, says, "OK, you're next," which is not what you want to hear from a postal worker. So, anyway, I mail the story, and I run to the bus so I can cover this book club lunch in Crescent Heights. It's the new trend. Guilt-ridden, middle-class women, they read one book a week, then get together to discuss it. This week's book is Henry James's *Portrait of a Lady.* Well, I like Henry James as much as the next person, who doesn't enjoy a sentence without a verb. So I get there, and the house is perfect, the hostess is gorgeous, her daughters all have these British names like Prunella and Cressida and Crudite. And then we meet the other "gals," these beautrons with bone structure. You could open beer bottles with their cheekbones. They've had so much plastic surgery their mouths meet at the backs of their necks. And one of them, Dorothy, is obviously so hung over, she's wearing sunglasses *in*side. Anyway, we sit down for lunch, which is low-fat cottage cheese and iced tea laced with, like, acid and PCBs, and then we go into the library, which my hostess points out has been organized by subject; I sense there's something fishy when I see they've got *Death of a Salesman* in with the murder mysteries. Then we sit in a circle and our hostess starts to give us background on Henry James, how he was from an important literary family, how he was an expatriate, how he was a "confirmed bachelor." Then we start in on the book, and I'm taking notes when about ten minutes into the discussion, the hostess comes out with the following. "I just didn't think Osmond was handsome." And they all nod, and she says, "Yes, Isabel's obsession is understandable in it's *context*, but if you'd seen him in that movie where he kept trying to kill Clint Eastwood and the president you just knew he was trouble from the get-go." And I realized . . . they're talking about John Malkovich. And I know I should keep my mouth shut, but frankly I've had a few Thunderbird Ice Teas myself, and I blurt out: "You didn't read the book! You're talking about *the movie*!" And they stare at me like I've gutted a deer on the rug. And one of them, the one in the sunglasses, Dorothy, raises her hand and says, "I didn't see the movie, but I must say I liked the first side much better than the second." She had listened to the audio book version. I say: "You can't talk about novels you saw at the movies or heard in the car! Besides which, Henry James was not a 'Confirmed Bachelor,' he was a closet queen who had his first sexual encounter with the future Chief Justice of the United States Supreme Court Oliver Wendall Holmes who set him on the homosexual path for life. Why do you think they called him The Magnificent Yankee? And another thing, *Dorothy*, just because you listened to the audiotape, don't think you're better than the rest of them! A book is meant to be READ! You have to look at it. You have to absorb the type face. A work of literature is meant for the eyes!" And then there's this long pause, and the hostess says: "Dorothy is blind." *(Beat.)* After that the discussion kind of petered out. Next week they're doing *Remembrance of Things Past.* Audio Books has a tape that erases itself as you listen to it. *(To Arno.)* How was your day?

What Corbin Knew

Jeffrey Hatcher

Scene: A VIP hospitality suite in a skybox high up in the entertainment complex of a large second-tier American city

Serio-comic

Margo (40ish), suburban housewife whose husband has just confessed to having an affair.

Here, Margo angrily confronts her husband, who has falsely led her to believe that he's having an affair with one of his students.

MARGO: Most women, if they thought for fifteen years that their husband was faithful, that he loved them, that he respected them, and then started to teach some phony-baloney writing class and started molding the work of all these talented writers with all their original voices and their novel narrative devices and had to have coffee with them after class, maybe a drink, a walk— and, oh yes, none of these talented voices are men, no *low, gruff* talented voices, just *high, chirpy* ones—and none of them are old or even middle-aged or fat or homely, all these original, vivid, talented, novel voices happen to be *really hot looking*. And then if most women had to listen to him one night while he explained that he was in love with one of his students, some scrawny, little exposed nerve from Sarah Lawrence who is "trying to make the move from journalism to fiction," like that's *hard*, like "Wo! She *was* a potato farmer, *now* she's trying to move into micro-surgery!" Come on! *(Pause.)* And then you start complaining why don't I talk about politics and books and art, and why aren't I ambitious, and why don't I work at some cool little alterative weekly where I can write pretentious, obscure can't-give-a-fucks and have lots of free time to be neurotic and complain about my writing and my dead-above-the-neck husband who's too stupid to notice that his wife is in love with her extension course teacher!

When Will I Dance

Claire Braz-Valentine

Scene: The studio of Mexican artist, Frida Kahlo

Dramatic

Frida Kahlo (30–50), severely crippled in her youth, yet quick and graceful, is an artist married to Diego Rivera, the famous muralist.

Haunted by pain and loss, Frida here describes her yearning to have a child.

FRIDA: OK, let's take a look at you. Juanita, you need a right eye, black and shiny. Maria needs hair. This time with curls Maria and blond. We'll make you a gringa! *(Leans forward to "listen" to Maria.)* Such language! Shame on you! Since you put it that way you can have black hair Maria. And little Laura needs a left arm, and Carmen has no shoes. Gloria needs a dress. Now that should do it. Don't look so sad all of you. By this time next week you will be gorgeous. *(Spins around to face mirror, picks flower, and places it in her braids.)* I will make you beautiful and then all the little boy dolls will want you, will think you luscious—delicious. *(Admires herself in mirror.)* They will make eyes at you from their shelves at night. When I finish with you, all those little boys will have hard pants all the time! *(Laughs.)* What a bunch of stupid shits they are! *(Still to the dolls.)* Listen to me ladies, first thing you have to know about men is that they are just plain suckers for beauty and the more beautiful you are, the bigger the bitch you can be. If you are ugly, you've got to be nice all the time. Now isn't that boring? But if you are a beauty, you can be bad . . . very, very bad and the worse you are the more men are enchanted by you. It doesn't take much to be beautiful. Most of it's just pretending you are already. Men fall for it all the time. Think about this little cotton heads, *(And to rubber doll.)* and you too little rubber head, if you are smart and you think you're beautiful, every man will want you. Now what could be simpler or more fun than that? And don't try to tell me women are the same. Women certainly don't fall in love with beauty or I wouldn't be in love with you know who. Now that's the truth! *(Lovingly places dolls one by one in the basket and finally picks up the rubber doll and sets it beside her on the bed, as in painting* Me and My Doll.*)(To audience.)* You know one thing people like to write about me? They say the reason I love dolls is because I can't have children. Those words cut me like knives. *(Pause.) (Sarcastically.)* What tremendous insight! Who are they to know? Who are they to know this emptiness, this hollow aching my flesh feels for the warmth and softness of my own baby? My own child. I had several *(Touches abdomen.)* in here. Perfect little babies. But there is something not right with me. One of my babies was actually here in my hand, in this palm. I touched it. It was no bigger than a little bug. So much blood, but I still felt so . . . so full and then our little baby, our beautiful little Mexican baby came out of me and I was suddenly hollow again, like wind could blow through my vagina and out my eyes and mouth. My doctors say no. They say I could not have possibly seen the baby, it was too small. What do they know about what a woman sees? A woman who is a mother one second then empty the next? What do they know with their scalpels and shovels? What do any of you know?

Women Behind the Walls

Claire Braz-Valentine

Scene: A California state prison

Dramatic

Nicki (20s), a prostitute and drug user. She is a return offender—very pretty and fast-talking.

Here, touch Nicki recalls one of her most unusual customers.

NICKI: Look at us. I mean, shit! You know the old saying, There's nothing worse than a woman drunk? Well there's something worse, a woman prisoner. A whore who's a prisoner, a black whore who's a prisoner and a drug addict. That's worse. Women are supposed to be all grace and loveliness, comfort and nurturing, gentle and soft. One time I had a regular John. Old guy. Nothing special. But I used to go to his room when he was in town. Good hotel, uptown. And after I gave him what he wanted I would always go into the bathroom and clean up. And underneath the towel on the towel bar, there was always $200. Just sticking out there so I knew I was suppose to see it. I took it. I always took it. Until one time I didn't. You know, I was getting to know the guy. Sort of feeling sorry for him in a way I guess. I didn't want to steal his money anymore. It just didn't feel right to me. The next time I visited him, as soon as I walked in the door, he slugged me right across the face, and said, "Don't you ever again feel that you're too good to steal my money. It's there for you to steal it." *(Pause.)* Sugar and spice and everything nice. How far we have fallen from grace.

Women Behind the Walls

Claire Braz-Valentine

Scene: A California state prison

Dramatic

Valdetta (20s), an African-American single mother, fiercely independent. Her neglect of her child led to tragedy and imprisonment.

Here, grieving Valdetta tells the sorrowful tale of her son's death.

VALDETTA: It was late, around 10 PM. We had a long day and he was tired. He was sound asleep. I had to go to the store to get some things for breakfast. I didn't want to wake him. It was just a block away and it was freezing out. I threw on my coat and ran down the three flights of stairs and down the street. When I got to the store I grabbed some milk and cereal and fruit. And there was a lady there in front of me, arguing with the clerk. I got nervous. I almost put the groceries down and ran home. *(Sobs.)* Oh God how I wish I had. But I waited another few minutes, and paid the clerk and raced out. I was halfway up the block when I remembered the candle. Our building is old and some of the lights don't work. I remember covering him. I remember seeing his face, his beautiful face, sleeping, seeing his face in the candlelight. *(Terror at memory.)* The candle I had left the candle. It suddenly was as if I was in a dream. I was running but couldn't move fast enough. I reached the apartment and started climbing the stairs and then I smelled the smoke. The awful smell. *(Frantic.)* I remember screaming his name. David. David. Over and over, knowing I shouldn't have left him alone, and the stairs going on forever, then the key, the key getting stuck in the rusty old lock and the smoke coming out. I remember the flames on the wall, the drapes and I ran to him, screaming, "Oh God please save my son, my baby."

(She picks up a bar and sits on the stage sobbing uncontrollably, the bar across her lap. Rosa goes over, strokes her hair. Comforts her.)

But I saved him. I saved my baby. And everything was going to be fine. Everything was going to be alright. But the Fire Department called Children's Services and they took him. They took my baby. And they put me in here.

Women Behind the Walls

Claire Braz-Valentine

Scene: A California state prison

Dramatic

Ellen (48), serving time for the attempted murder of her husband.

Ellen has been systematically brutalized by her husband for many years. Here, she explains how she came to be married to a monster.

ELLEN: My mother and father didn't want me to marry him but I did anyway. My sisters said I was crazy. He was so much older than me. He said he just wanted a companion to travel with. He traveled all over the world. He said it would be easier if we were married, but he promised me he wasn't interested in sex, that we wouldn't consummate the marriage. My parents and sisters were right. I was young and stupid. The first night in a foreign county he raped me. The next morning he never said anything about it, except that he took my passport and he never returned it to me. He took me to a jewelry store and bought me a beautiful bracelet, solid gold. That night I slept on my stomach. I was just about asleep when I heard him come into the room. I don't even want to tell you what he did. I was so ashamed that I never told anyone. I didn't tell anyone of the years of abuse, of how he would always tell me I was ugly. I was never pretty. I was always stupid. I kept going back to the dentist all the time because he broke my bridge so often. Once I tried to jump out of a fifteen-story window in a hotel. He caught me by the feet. He told me that if I was going to die he would be the one to kill me. He said he would kill my mother, my son, my whole family. He had guns all over the house, under his pillow, under the couch. I was so ashamed. That's how denial begins. It's born in shame. My son was born in shame, but I told myself I stayed in the marriage for him. What an awful burden on such small shoulders.

Zoë's Story

Nancy Wright

Scene: Northern Ohio

Serio-comic

Zoë (30s), an exotic dancer and substance abuser who dreams of becoming a writer.

When her shrink asks what substance she's currently abusing, outspoken Zoë makes the following reply.

ZOË: I like that term, "substances." It sounds so scientific. Let's see. Do I have to include every single chemical? You know, like hair spray, nail polish, deodorant? Eyeliner, mascara, eye shadow, lipstick—oh–oh—I almost forgot: nail polish remover!—that one's deadly!—shampoo, conditioner, hair-coloring—definitely habit-forming—styling spritz, styling gel, mousse—not the animal—soap, sunblock, Alpha-Hydroxy—I don't know what's in that, but it can't be good for you . . . God. This is going to be a really long list. But what can I do, Doc? Exotic dancers gotta use, or they lose. Lose their looks, I mean. Can you relate?

(Dr. Shapiro regards her seriously. Zoë reacts with a shudder.)

Whoa! Old evil eye is back. Well, two can play at this game. *(She stares back.)* I got nothing to hide: I still smoke. I still drink— a lot—I love it. I snort the occasional coke, usually when some nice man wants to share with me. I smoke dope most nights before I go to work or just to relax when I'm home alone watching daytime TV. *Oprah* is brilliant when you're stoned. And once in a while, if I need to work extra jobs or lose a few pounds, I do some speed. Oh, and I take Valium when I can get it. Can you write me a scrip for that, Dr. S?

[DR. SHAPIRO: Is that all?]

ZOË: Not quite. I don't know how to tell you this, Doc, but sometimes . . . sometimes I do *chocolate*. Lots and lots of *chocolate*. Seriously—I may be a *chocoholic*. What do *you* think?

Zoë's Story

Nancy Wright

Scene: Northern Ohio

Dramatic

Zoë (30s), an exotic dancer and substance abuser who dreams of becoming a writer.

> Zoë has longed to become a writer, but life on the edge has destroyed all hopes of a literary career. Here, she is interviewed on the radio near the end of her short but dramatic life.

ZOË: Oh—are we back from commercial? Sorry. You wanted to know how long I've been dancing? Jesus— *(Conscious of her listening audience.)* I mean—Gee Whiz! Forever. Since I was eighteen. I'm almost thirty-six now, except I lie and say I'm thirty. *(Lightly, almost coyly, to someone out of sight out front, presumably the interviewer.)* People believe me. Sometimes. Too bad you can't stay in this business twenty-five or thirty years and retire with a gold watch and a pension and go live in Florida or Arizona. Oh well. I know now I won't ever be a writer. I can't make up stuff the way I always wanted to, and I sure don't want to write stuff down the way it really happens. But sometimes when I'm at work bored out of my mind, or when I'm lying in bed halfway between asleep and awake, I think I have a story to tell. Something about the way life works or doesn't work and what I wish for. Hell, maybe we all have a story to tell and you don't have to be a writer to tell it. Maybe you can find another way to pass it on so your story doesn't end when you do. So it maybe makes more sense to someone else than it did to you. I figure I've been lucky and unlucky in life, just like everybody else. My mix is different from yours, but who's to say what's harder or better? I've got a son who's gonna tell his story someday—he'll have a hell of a story to tell—and I've got two writer friends who bust a gut every day trying to tell other people's stories. Between the three of 'em, pieces of my story'll get told, for sure, and maybe that's enough. Maybe that's plenty. *(She has grown contemplative, quiet. She checks her watch.)* My time's about up—isn't it?

NOTE: These monologues are intended to be used for audition and class study; permission is not required to use the material for those purposes. However, if there is a paid performance of any of the monologues included in this book, please refer to the permissions acknowledgments below to locate the source who can grant permission for public performance.

A.B.C. or The Man in The Red Suit. Copyright 1999 by Leslie Bramm. Contact: Leslie Bramm. 185 East 80th Street #4W New York, NY 10021

The Adulterer. Copyright 1999 by Jussi Wahlgren. Reprinted by Permission of the Author For International Performing Rights contact: Charles Aerts Theatre Productions International Valeriusplein 20 1075 BH Amsterdam Holland 20-6732285 Represented in the United States by: Frank Tobin 213-661-3720 Or Contact: Jussi Wahlgren Kukkaniityntie 17 00900 Helsinki Finland

Alchemy. Copyright 2000 by L. S. Wilkinson Reprinted by Permission of the Author Contact: L. S. Wilkinson 100 Barnet Grove London E.2 7BJ UK 44 (02) 7739-6363

Are You All Right in There? Copyright 2000 by David-Matthew Barnes Reprinted by Permission of the Author Contact: The Dorothy Nickle Performing Arts Company 2221 West Giddings Street Chicago, IL 60625 Attention: Harriet Russell, Literary Department

Bad Buddhists. Copyright 1999 by Robert Vivian Reprinted by Permission of the Author Contact: Robert Vivian 4724 Davenport, #1 Omaha, NE 68132 (402) 553-7168

The Belles of The Mill. Copyright 1999 by Rachel Rubin Ladutke Reprinted by Permission of the Author Contact: Rachel Rubin Ladutke darling67@theatermail.net or www.geocities.com/darling1967

Officer Justice. Copyright 1999 by Janet Pound Reprinted by Permission of the Author Contact: Janet Pound 12924 Sherwood Huntington Woods, MI 48070

Party Store Prisoner. Copyright 1999 by Janet Pound Reprinted by Permission of the Author Contact: Janet Pound 12924 Sherwood Huntington Woods, MI 48070

The Power of Love. Copyright 1999 by Sebastian Michael Reprinted by Permission of The Rod Hall Agency, Ltd. Contact: Clare Barker, Author's Agent The Rod Hall Agency, Ltd 7 Goodge Place London W1D 1FL UK 171-637-0706 171-637-0807 – fax rod.hall@dial.pipex.com

The Quarterly. Copyright 1999 by Valerie von Rosenvinge Reprinted by Permission of the Author Contact: Valerie von Rosenvinge 77 Cliff Road Wellesley, MA 02481 (781) 237-0833

Rage Amongst Yourselves. Copyright 1999 by Amy Beth Arkawy Reprinted by Permission of the Author Contact: Amy Beth Arkawy 12 Elm Hill Drive Rye Brook, NY 10573

The Rim of The Wheel Copyright 1998, 2000 by Daphne R. Hull Reprinted by Permission of the Author Contact: Daphne R. Hull 230 West Lanvale Baltimore, MD 21217

The Serpent's Kiss. Copyright 2000 by Jocelyn Beard Reprinted by Permission of the Author Contact: Jocelyn Beard kitowski@computer.net

Shoes. Copyright 1999 by Sky Vogel Reprinted by Permission of the Author Contact: Sky Vogel 30 Evergreen Avenue Clifton Park, NY 12065

Small Mercies. Copyright 1999 by Heidi Decker Reprinted by Permission of the Author Contact: Heidi Decker 300 Vuemont Place #C106 Renton, WA 98056 HEDecker@aol.com

142